Contents

INTRODUCTION

The *Kruger Routes Self-Drive Companion* is a condensed version of the bigger, more comprehensive book *Kruger Self-Drive – Routes, Roads & Ratings* by the same authors. Use the comprehensive version to learn more about the area you are about to explore and take the travel companion with you as a handy guide and to make notes as you go.

PLAN YOUR TRIP

The sections designated for general tourist activities have an exceptional network of roads that access some of the best areas for game viewing in the park.

There are **12 main rest camps** and several private, bush and concession camps in the Kruger National Park.

The **routes** given in this book are the ones that **start and end at the main rest camps** and the roads that are accessible to all self-driving tourists in the park. The listed routes include only suggested prime routes. There are many other possibilities. Routes can be done clockwise or anti-clockwise and can be lengthened or shortened to

suit your own interests and available time. Use the road ratings and information to decide on your own routes. Lower-rated routes may be surprisingly good and high-rated routes may also be disappointing at times. Game sightings are mostly unpredictable. To find and watch is the challenge.

HOW TO PLAN YOUR ROUTE

- Study the area map.
- Decide between a morning drive (short or long) and/or afternoon drive (usually short) or day drive.
- Look at breakfast and/or lunch options or pack a picnic basket.
- Look at the recommended prime roads for the area.
- Read more about them to make informed decisions. (See the chapter on ROADS in the main *Kruger Self-Drive – Routes, Roads & Ratings*.)
- Locate the animal drinking places on the area map.
- Decide on your route by taking all the above into account.
- Make a quick calculation of the distance you plan to travel and divide by 25 km/h to determine the time you should set aside. For example, to cover a distance of 100 km you need to allow about four hours. Decide on your own 'via' roads.
- Four to five hours for a morning drive is more than enough. An afternoon drive would usually not exceed three hours. A day drive should not be more than 200–250 km. Allow time for relaxing at picnic sites or neighbouring camps.
- Covering too great a distance will leave you exhausted and inclined to break the speed limit.
- The suggested routes show only the main points, with a rough calculation of the time it would take for an unhurried game drive. Calculate approximate time, allowing for a picnic.

BE BUSHWISE

Be safe and stay in your vehicle unless you are at a place signposted as a 'get-out' point. Hanging out of the windows breaks the familiar outline of the vehicle and frightens animals away. They are comfortable with vehicles but not with people.

TIME OF DAY

- **Early risers** may encounter predators that spent the night on the warm tarred or sandy roads – especially in winter.
- **Hyena** are often seen returning to their dens and running along the road in the **early mornings**. They often den in culverts along the road.
- Predator activity is **at a minimum during midday periods** and even herbivores seek shade.
- **Cheetah** are diurnal and hunt during **any time of the day**. They prefer open spaces to run down their prey and avoid areas where they have to compete with lions.
- Look up into trees – you may have a pleasant surprise and spot a **leopard resting on a branch**.

Month	Entrance gates open	Camp gates open	All gates close
Jan	05:30	04:30	18:30
Feb	05:30	05:30	18:30
Mar	05:30	05:30	18:00
Apr	06:00	06:00	18:00
May	06:00	06:00	17:30
Jun	06:00	06:00	17:30
Jul	06:00	06:00	17:30
Aug	06:00	06:00	18:00
Sep	06:00	06:00	18:00
Oct	05:30	05:30	18:00
Nov	05:30	04:30	18:30
Dec	05:30	04:30	18:30

KNOWLEDGE OF THE LATEST SIGHTINGS

- Visit the **sightings board** at each camp – it will give you an indication of the latest and best sightings.
- Consult the **visitors' book** at reception.
- **Talk to people** and share knowledge of sightings.
- Many sightings are **fleeting glimpses** of predators and it is not always worth pursuing these.
- Predators with **young cubs or pups** tend to keep to a specific area for some time. Ask around.
- **Lions at a big kill** often take days to feed. Once they have had their fill, the scavengers arrive.
- **Denning animals** (such as hyena and wild dog) with young tend to stay in a specific area for a long time. Repeated sightings are almost a certainty.

SEASON

Years of **dry and wet cycles alternate** and influence the predator–prey relationships. During years of drought, predators flourish because animals tend to concentrate around the watering points, so it requires less energy to find prey. During a wet cycle, plant feeders increase in condition and numbers because of lush vegetation and available water sources. Predators find it more difficult to hunt successfully in these conditions since their prey is widely dispersed.

- **Rainfall** in the previous summer months determines the onset of the **wildebeest and zebra migrations** from south to north and back.
- The **first rains** usually occur in spring (Oct/Nov) and the wet season lasts until about April. Occasional and unexpected showers may, however, occur in the dry season.
- After a good summer season, the grass may be high and the bush quite dense. This makes it **difficult to spot game**.
- During **mid-winter** when **mornings** are chilly, there tends to be less animal activity until it warms up.
- **Winter afternoons** are usually very productive.
- The **lambing season** starts at the onset of summer (Nov/Dec).

AT WATERHOLES

In summer or after rain, there may be enough water in **temporary pans further away** from regular waterholes. The best time to watch game at watering points will be in the dry season, which usually peaks in September/October.

- **Big herds** appear at waterholes only around **mid-morning** – buffalo, zebra, wildebeest, waterbuck, kudu, giraffe and impala.
- **Mid-afternoon** is excellent for sightings of elephant drinking and bathing. White rhino may also appear.
- On **hot days,** rhino, buffalo, warthog and elephant often wallow in the mud.
- **Black rhino** usually drink **during early to late evening** and are frequently spotted on night drives.

WEATHER CONDITIONS

- Game drives are usually **good on cool, heavily overcast** days. In such weather, even cats may hunt right through the day.
- Although **leopards** are mainly nocturnal, they are often seen during the day, especially on **cool, drizzly** days.
- When the grass is long and wet, **predators prefer to keep dry** and **use the roads** when on the move.
- Most animals are very **skittish on windy days** and avoid coming out into the open.

NIGHT DRIVES

- **Self-drive** after gate-closing time is **not allowed** but **guided night drives** in a park vehicle can be booked at reception.
- Expect to **see any of the following** on a night drive: civet, genet, porcupine, white-tailed mongoose, honey badger, aardvark, pangolin, African wild cat, black-footed cat (at Punda Maria), black rhino, the Big Five and hyena.

KRUGER MAP

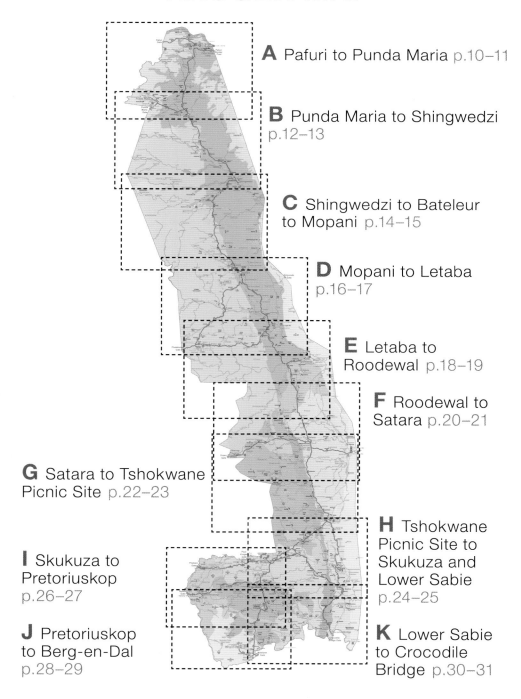

A Pafuri to Punda Maria p.10–11

B Punda Maria to Shingwedzi p.12–13

C Shingwedzi to Bateleur to Mopani p.14–15

D Mopani to Letaba p.16–17

E Letaba to Roodewal p.18–19

F Roodewal to Satara p.20–21

G Satara to Tshokwane Picnic Site p.22–23

H Tshokwane Picnic Site to Skukuza and Lower Sabie p.24–25

I Skukuza to Pretoriuskop p.26–27

J Pretoriuskop to Berg-en-Dal p.28–29

K Lower Sabie to Crocodile Bridge p.30–31

LEGEND

🛏	Concession accommodation
🚙	Get-out point
👥	Hide
🍴	Lookout point
▯	Monument
⛱	Picnic spot
⊖	No entry
⊖	No entry except residents
Ⓖ	Public gate
⬤	Bushveld camp
📷	Caravan site
🛏	Rest camp
▲	Tented camp
🚶	Trails camp
ⓦ	Waterholes/pans/drinking troughs
⥤	Dams
—	Rivers
⌃	Mountains/hills
----	Private road
=	Tourist gravel road
━	Tourist tar road

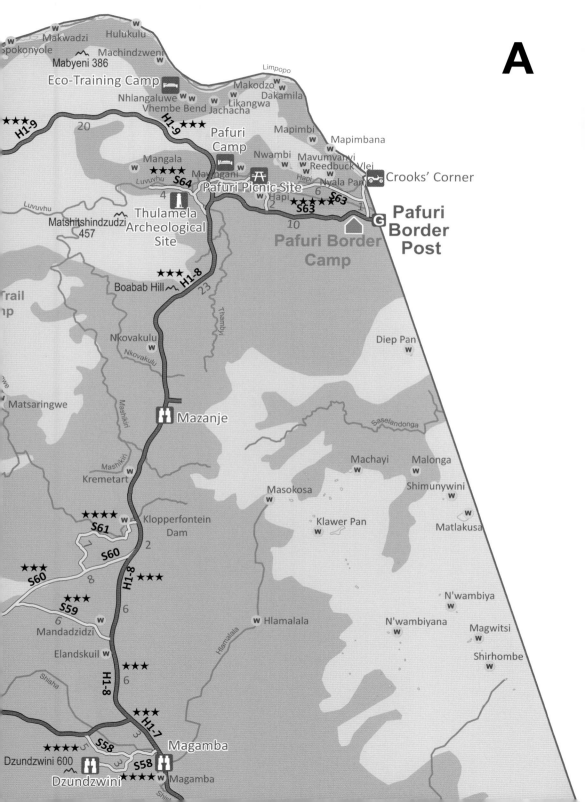

A

B

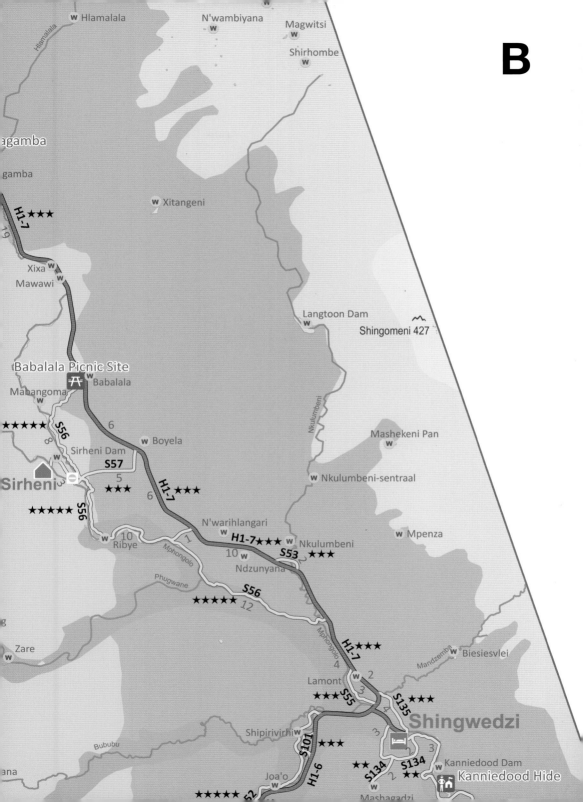

W Hlamalala

N'wambiyana

W Magwitsi

W Shirhombe

agamba

gamba

W Xitangeni

H1-7 ★★★

Xixa W
Mawawi W

Langtoon Dam
W

Shingomeni 427

Babalala Picnic Site

Babalala

Mabangoma

★★★★★ S56

8

Sirheni Dam

Sirheni

S57

6

★★★ ★★★★★ S56

5

6 H1-7 ★★★

W Boyela

Mashekeni Pan

W Nkulumbeni-sentraal

W Mpenza

10
Ribye W

Mphongolo

1

N'warihlangari
W

H1-7 ★★★ W Nkulumbeni

10 W Ndzunyana

S53 ★★★

Phugwane

S56

★★★★★ 12

Zare
W

Mphongolo

H1-7 ★★★

4

Mandzemba W Biesiesvlei

Lamont
W 2

★★★ S55

3

S135 ★★★

4

Shingwedzi

Shipirivirhi W

3

S101 ★★★

H1-6

Joa'o

★★★★★ 52

2

S134

★★

S134

2 ★★

W Kanniedood Dam

Kanniedood Hide

Mashagadzi

Bububu

Ntomeni No. 1 Ntomeni No. 2 N'waminyulu No. 1

N'waminyulu No. 2

Bububu Awie-se-dam

Bububu Qivi ra Machangana

Nshenhene

ariyeta
ncession

hunshatinjovo

Maketekete Shikokola

Phonda Hills 404

Basabasa Nkayeni

★★★★★ S5

Shingwedzi

Nkayini Silwervis Dam Tsh

Bateleur Tshanga Lo

Rooibosrant Dam Tshanga

Mahlambandlopfu 7

Cibe Sha Tol

Mahlatuba

Nalatsi

O

Ntomeni

Sh

Tshombyeni S1

★★

Byashishi

Phiri

Little Letaba Mahubyeni

C

Shingwedzi

S135 ★★★

S101 ★★★

Shipirivirhi w

H1-6

S134 ★★
★★

S134
★★ w

Joa'o w

Kanniedood Dam

Kanniedood Hide

★★★★★ S52

Mashagadzi

15

Shingwedzi

S50 ★★★★

16

Red Rocks

20 w Mimondzweni

Mfenheni w

Gadzingwe

2

Mkakweni

Shingwedzi S52

Tshilonde

★★★★★

8

Dipeni w

H1-6 ★★★

Krapkuil Dam w Nkokodzi

33

Dzombo w

Gans Pan

t

Dzombo West

Nyawutsi
Hide

S54 ★★★

H1-6 ★★★

Dzombo

Dzombo East

Nyawutsi

10

S103 ★★

Kumba

1 w

Olifantsbad Pan

Hlamvu w

S144 ★★

19

Grootvlei Dam ☆

N'wambu

★★★★ S50

★★★ S142

Pan w

Shibavantsengele 482

Eendrag

6

N'wambu Pan

Shibavantsengele
Lookout

Tropic of
Capricorn
Cairn

4

S144 ★★

S143

Shibavantsengele 482

Welgelegen Pan w

w Grysbok

★★★

16 w Tihongonyeni

Shilowa 382

24

Shidayangwenya w

13

Nshawu

17

w Frazersrus

H1-6 ★★★

w Bowkerskop

w Nshawu (Nxawu) Dam

Bowkerskop
378

Pioneer
Dam

Tsendze

2

5 w Nshawu (Nxawu) No. 3

Pioneer Hide

Mopani

2 3 w Mooiplaas

w Nshawu (Nxawu) No. 2

S142

★★★★

★★ S146

Shipandani

S50 4

S50 ★★★★

H1-6

Kumba

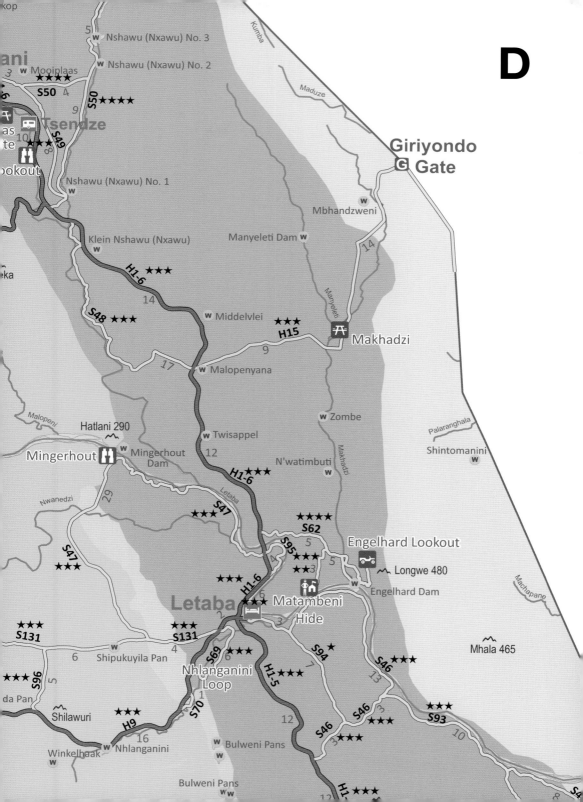

D

kop

5   w   Nshawu (Nxawu) No. 3

3   w   Nshawu (Nxawu) No. 2

ani

w   Mooiplaas ★★★★

S50   4

S50 ★★★★

9

Tsendze

Kumba

Maduze

Giriyondo
G Gate

S49

as

10

ookout

8

Nshawu (Nxawu) No. 1

w

Mbhandzweni

ka

Klein Nshawu (Nxawu)

w

Manyeleti Dam   w

14

H1-6 ★★★

14

S48 ★★★

w   Middelvlei   ★★★

H15

9

w   Malopenyana

17

🅿   **Makhadzi**

Malopeni

Hatlani 290

w   Zombe

Palaranghala

Mingerhout 🏠   w   Mingerhout
        Dam

w   Twisappel

12

N'watimbuti
w

Shintomanini

Nwanedzi

29

H1-6 ★★★

Letaba

S47

S47 ★★★

w

★★★

★★★★

S62

5

Engelhard Lookout

Machapane

S95 ★★★

★★ 3

5

🚐

w

Longwe 480

Engelhard Dam

4   **H1-6** ★★★

6

Letaba   ★★★

🏠   **Matambeni**
        Hide

3

Mhala 465

★★★

S131

★★★

S131

2

S94 ★

S46 ★★★

6   Shipukuyila Pan   4

S69   6   ★★★

7

13

★★★ **S96**

5

Nhlanganini
Loop

H1-5 ★★★

12

S46

3

★★★ **S93**

da Pan

1

S70

★★★

S46 ★★★

10

★★★

H9

12

S46

Shilawuri

16   **Nhlanganini**

w   Bulweni Pans

3   ★★★

Winkelhaak

w

w

Bulweni Pans

w w

H1- ★★★

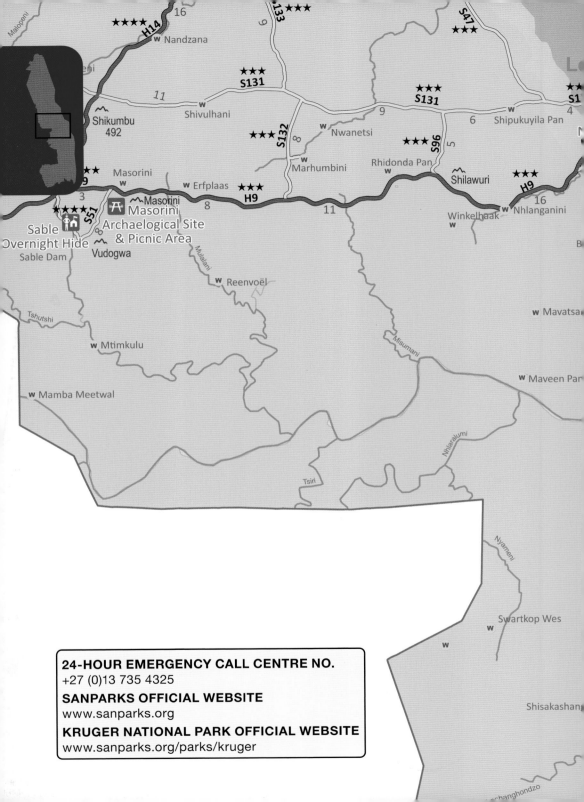

★★★★ H14 16
Nandzana
★★★ S133
S47 ★★★
★★★

★★★ S131
★★★ S131
S1 ★★
11
9 4
Shivulhani
Shipukuyila Pan
Shikumbu 492
★★★ S132 Nwanetsi
8
★★★ S96
N
★★ Masorini
Marhumbini
Rhidonda Pan
Shilawuri ★★★ H9
9 Erfplaas ★★★ H9
16
8 11 Nhlanganini
★★★★ S51 Masorini ⛺ Masorini Archaelogical Site & Picnic Area
Winkelhaak
3
Sable Overnight Hide
Vudogwa
Sable Dam

Reenvoël
Tshutshi
Mavatsa
Mtimkulu
Misumani
Maveen Par
Mamba Meetwal
Nhlaralumi
Tsiri
Nyameni
Swartkop Wes
Shisakashan

24-HOUR EMERGENCY CALL CENTRE NO.
+27 (0)13 735 4325
SANPARKS OFFICIAL WEBSITE
www.sanparks.org
KRUGER NATIONAL PARK OFFICIAL WEBSITE
www.sanparks.org/parks/kruger

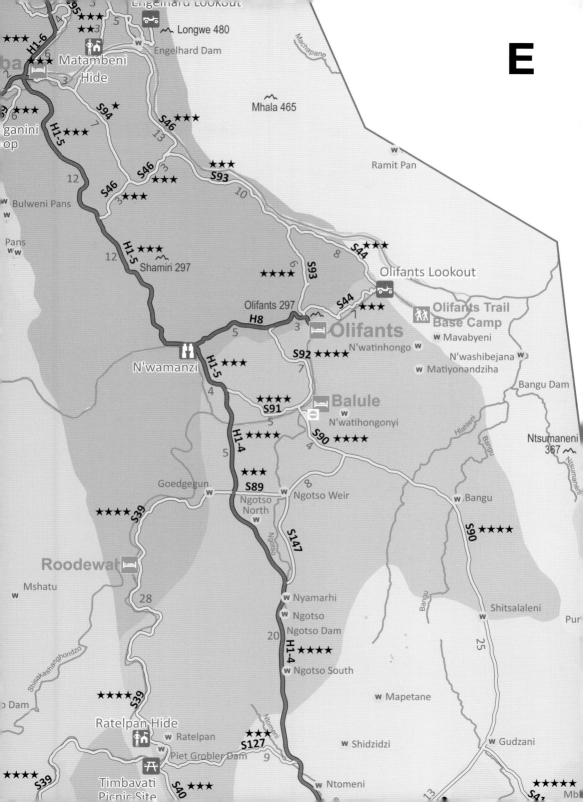

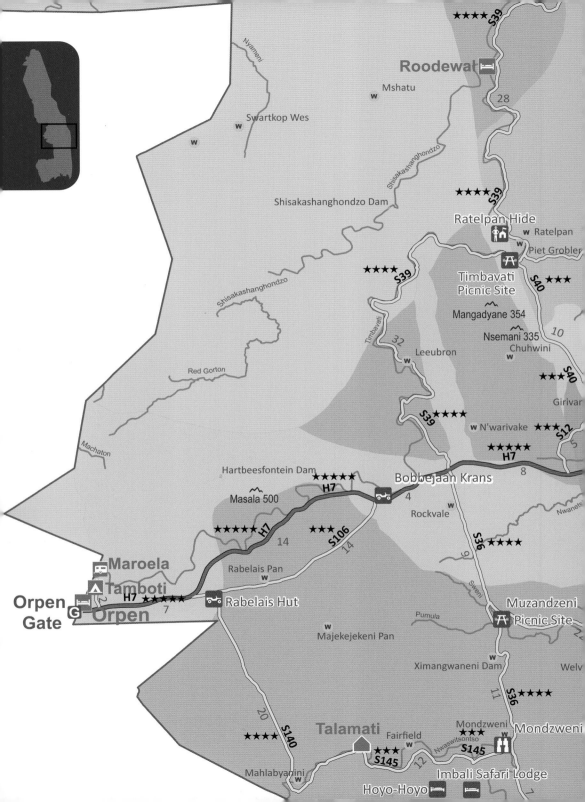

Roodewal ★★★★ S39

Mshatu w

28

Swartkop Wes

w

Shisakashanghondzo Dam

Nyameni

★★★★ S39

Ratelpan Hide
w Ratelpan

Piet Grobler

★★★★ S39

Timbavati
Picnic Site

S40 ★★★

Mangadyane 354

Nsemani 335

Chuhwini w

Shisakashanghondzo

Red Gorton

Timbavati

32

Leeubron

w

★★★ S40

Girivar

S39 ★★★★

w N'warivake ★★★ S12

S5

★★★★★
H7

Machaton

Hartbeesfontein Dam

★★★★★

H7

Masala 500

Bobbejaan Krans

4

Rockvale w

8

Nwanets

★★★★★ H7

14

★★★ S106

14

S36

9

★★★★

Sweni

Maroela

Rabelais Pan
w

Tamboti

Orpen
Gate

Orpen

H7
2

★★★★★

7

Rabelais Hut

Muzandzeni
Picnic Site

Pumula

Majekejekeni Pan w

Ximangwaneni Dam w

Welv

11 S36 ★★★★

20 S140

Talamati

Fairfield

Mondzweni
★★★

Mondzweni

Nwaswitsontso

S145

★★★★ S140

★★★ S145

Mahlabyanini w

12

Imbali Safari Lodge

Hoyo-Hoyo

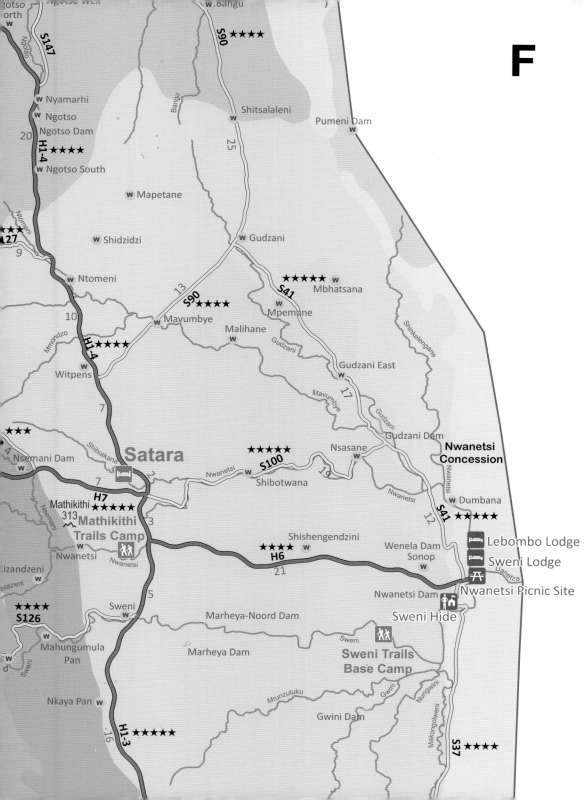

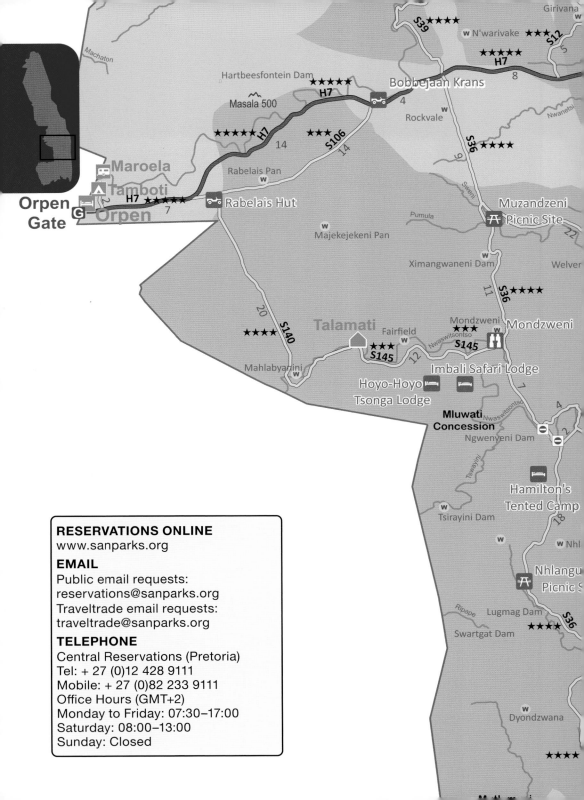

Girivana

S39 ★★★★

w N'warivake ★★★ S12

★★★★★
H7

Hartbeesfontein Dam ★★★★★

Machaton

Bobbejaan Krans

Masala 500 H7

4

Rockvale w

Nwanetsi

★★★★★ H7

★★★ S106

S36

★★★★

14

14

9

Maroela

Sweni

Rabelais Pan w

Pumula

Muzandzeni

22

Orpen
Gate

Tamboti

H7 ★★★★★

Orpen

7

Rabelais Hut

Majekejekeni Pan w

Picnic Site

Ximangwaneni Dam w

Welver

2

11 S36 ★★★★

Mondzweni ★★★

Mondzweni

20

S140 ★★★★

Talamati

Fairfield w

Nwaswitsontso

S145

★★★ S145

12

Imbali Safari Lodge

Mahlabyanini w

7

Hoyo-Hoyo
Tsonga Lodge

Mluwati
Concession

Nwaswitsontso

4

Ngwenyeni Dam

2

Tawayini

Hamilton's
Tented Camp

18

Tsirayini Dam w

w

w Nhl

Nhlangu
Picnic S

Ripape

Lugmag Dam

S36

Swartgat Dam

★★★★

Dyondzwana w

★★★★

RESERVATIONS ONLINE
www.sanparks.org

EMAIL
Public email requests:
reservations@sanparks.org
Traveltrade email requests:
traveltrade@sanparks.org

TELEPHONE
Central Reservations (Pretoria)
Tel: + 27 (0)12 428 9111
Mobile: + 27 (0)82 233 9111
Office Hours (GMT+2)
Monday to Friday: 07:30–17:00
Saturday: 08:00–13:00
Sunday: Closed

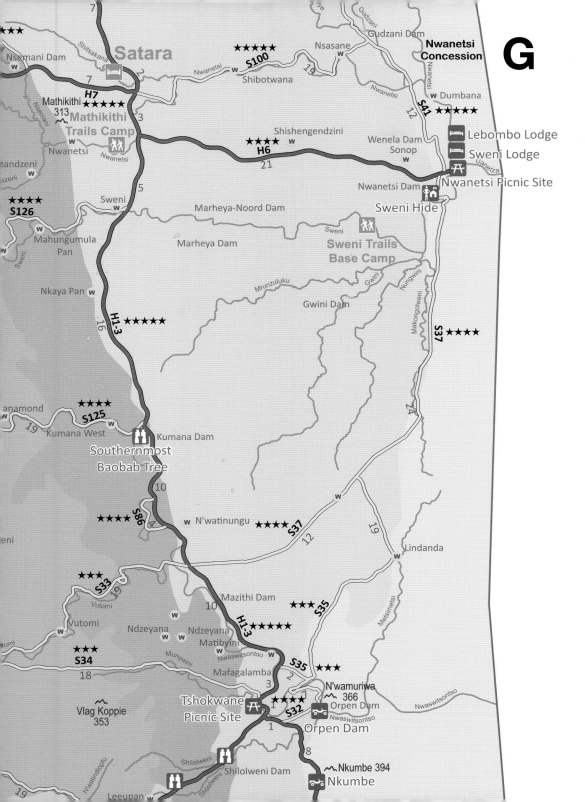

G

★★★

Nsemani Dam

★★★★★ S100
Nsasane

Gudzani Dam

Nwanetsi Concession

Satara

Nwanetsi

Shibotwana

Dumbana

S41 ★★★★★

H7

Mathikithi ★★★★★
313

Mathikithi Trails Camp

Nwanetsi

Shishengendzini

★★★★ H6

21

Wenela Dam Sonop

Lebombo Lodge

Sweni Lodge

Nwanetsi Picnic Site

★★★★ S126

Sweni

5

Marheya-Noord Dam

Nwanetsi Dam

Sweni Hide

Mahungumula Pan

Marheya Dam

Sweni Trails Base Camp

Nkaya Pan

16

H1-3 ★★★★★

Mrunzuluku

Gwini Dam

Nungwini

Makongolweni

S37 ★★★★

24

★★★★ S125

anamond

19

Kumana West

Kumana Dam

Southernmost Baobab Tree

10

★★★★ S86

eni

N'watinungu ★★★★ S37

12

19

Lindanda

★★★ S33

Vutomi

19

Mazithi Dam

★★★ S35

Metsimetsi

Vutomi

Ndzeyana

Ndzeyana
Matibyini

10

H1-3 ★★★★★

★★★ S34

18

Munywini

Nwaswitsontso

S35 ★★★

★★★

Mafagalamba

N'wamuriwa 366

Nwaswitsontso

Vlag Koppie 353

Tshokwane Picnic Site

3

★★★★

1 S32

Orpen Dam

Orpen Dam

1

Nwaswitsontso

Shiloweni

8

Nkumbe 394

Shiloweni Dam

Nkumbe

19

Leeupan

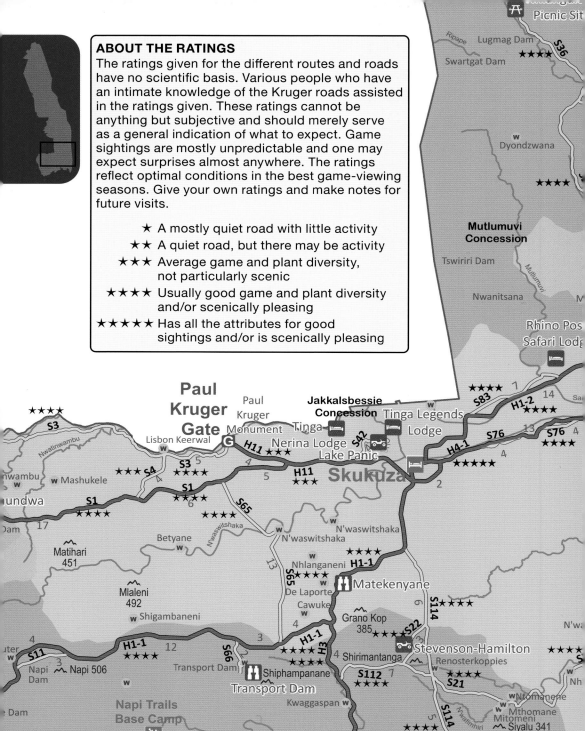

ABOUT THE RATINGS

The ratings given for the different routes and roads have no scientific basis. Various people who have an intimate knowledge of the Kruger roads assisted in the ratings given. These ratings cannot be anything but subjective and should merely serve as a general indication of what to expect. Game sightings are mostly unpredictable and one may expect surprises almost anywhere. The ratings reflect optimal conditions in the best game-viewing seasons. Give your own ratings and make notes for future visits.

★ A mostly quiet road with little activity

★★ A quiet road, but there may be activity

★★★ Average game and plant diversity, not particularly scenic

★★★★ Usually good game and plant diversity and/or scenically pleasing

★★★★★ Has all the attributes for good sightings and/or is scenically pleasing

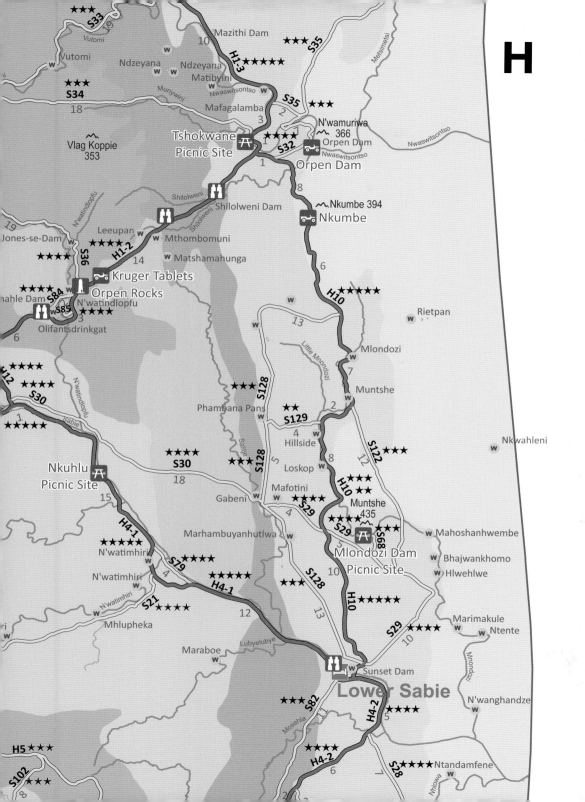

LEGEND

🛏	Concession accommodation	🛏	Rest camp
🚙	Get-out point	⛺	Tented camp
👫	Hide	🥾	Trails camp
🔭	Lookout point	w	Waterholes/pans/drinking troughs
🏛	Monument		
🪑	Picnic spot	◁	Dams
⊖	No entry	—	Rivers
⊜	No entry except residents	⌒	Mountains/hills
Ⓖ	Public gate	ˋˋˋ	Private road
🏠	Bushveld camp	═	Tourist gravel road
🚐	Caravan site	▬	Tourist tar road

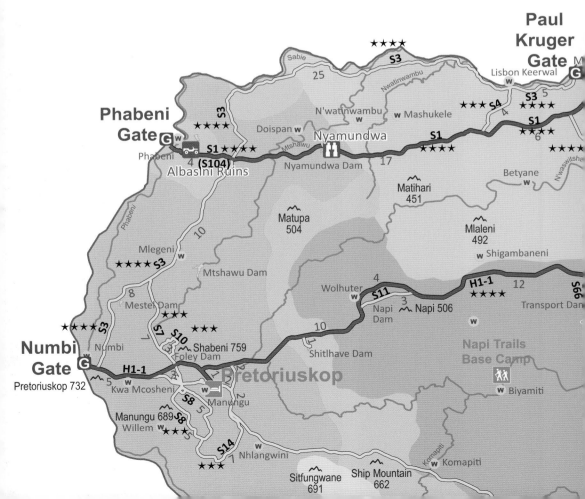

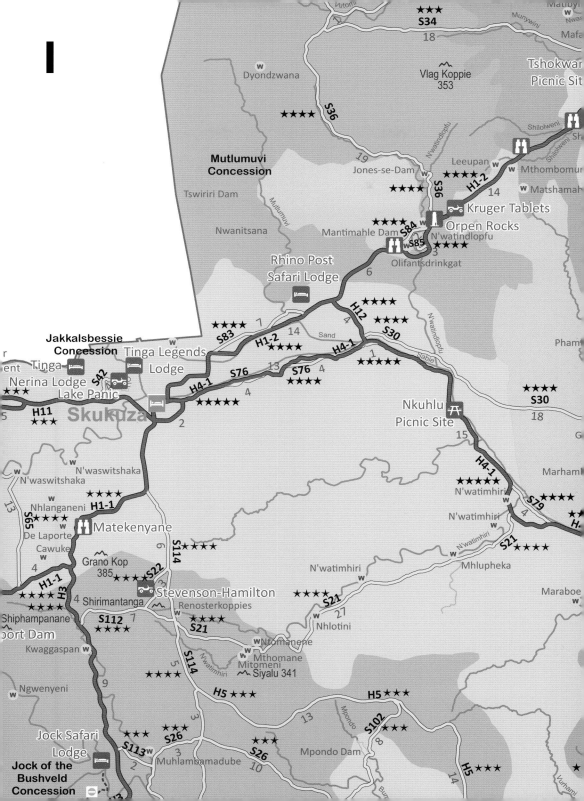

Mlegeni
★★★★ S3 w
Mtshawu Dam

8
Mestel Dam
★★★
★★★
S7 S10
★ S3
S3
Numbi
Shabeni 759
3
Foley Dam
H1-1
5
Kwa Mcosheni
Manungu
S8 w
Manungu 689 S8
Willem w ★★★
S14
Nhlangwini
★★★

Wolhuter
S11
4
w
Napi Dam
Napi 506
H1-1 ★★★★ 12
Transport D
w
Napi Trails
Base Camp
w Biyamiti

Shigambaneni
w

10
Shitlhave Dam

Pretoriuskop

Sitfungwane 691
Ship Mountain 662
Komapiti
w Komapiti

H2-2 ★★★
38
Mitomeni

Newu 666
Mangake 697

Newu Dam
Reno
R

Stolsnek Dam
Mlambane
w
Ampie

Wolhuter Trails Base Camp
Mavukani

Nsikazi
Mnyeleni
Bushman Trails Base Camp

Matjulu 627
Matjulu w
8 ★★★★
S110
Berg-en-Dal D
Berg-en-Dal
Matjulu

Maqili 674

S110
10
★★★★
T

w Nsikazi Meetwal
Khandzalive 839

Male
Rest

J

Grano Kop 385 ★★★★ **S22**

14

N'watimhiri

Mhlupheka

H1-1 **H3** ★★★★ Shirimantanga 4

Stevenson-Hamilton
Renosterkoppies

★★★★ **S21** 27

Nhlotini

Shiphampanane

S112 ★★★★ 7 **S21**

Ntomanene

sport Dam

Kwaggaspan

★★★★ **S114** 5

Nwatimhiri

Mthomane
Mitomeni
Siyalu 341

Ngwenyeni 9

H5 ★★★

H5 ★★★

S102 ★★★

Mpondo

Jock Safari Lodge ★★★ **S26** ★★★

S113 2 3

S26 ★★★ 10

Mpondo Dam

8

H5 ★★★

Jock of the Bushveld Concession **H3** Muhlambamadube

14

Bume

S23 11 10 Biyamiti

Mahlamarisa

★★★ **S26** 10

Watergat

S114 ★★★★

★★★ **S108** ★★★ **H5**

12

Biyamiti Weir

18

Kacagisenga
Gayisenga

4 6

Afsaal Trader's Rest

Blinkwater

Bume

Gomond

H3 Jock

S114 ★★★★ ★★★★

★★★★ **S25**

Gomo

erpan ★★★ **H3**

H2-2 8 **S114** 7

Lwakahle

Biyamiti Bushveld Camp

S25 12 **S25** ★★

Hi

9

5

Lwakahle Concession

★★★★ **S118**

★★★★

5

Lukimbi Safari Lodge

Crocodile

Hipp

N'wankwimbi **S119** 6

★★★★★ **S114**

Gardenia Hide

★★★★ **S25**

★★ **S120**

S121 ★★★ 6 2

S25 18

Van Graan Hectorspruit Meetwal

H3 ★★★★

S114 ★★★★ 6

S110

2

Hill

Malelane Gate G

rp

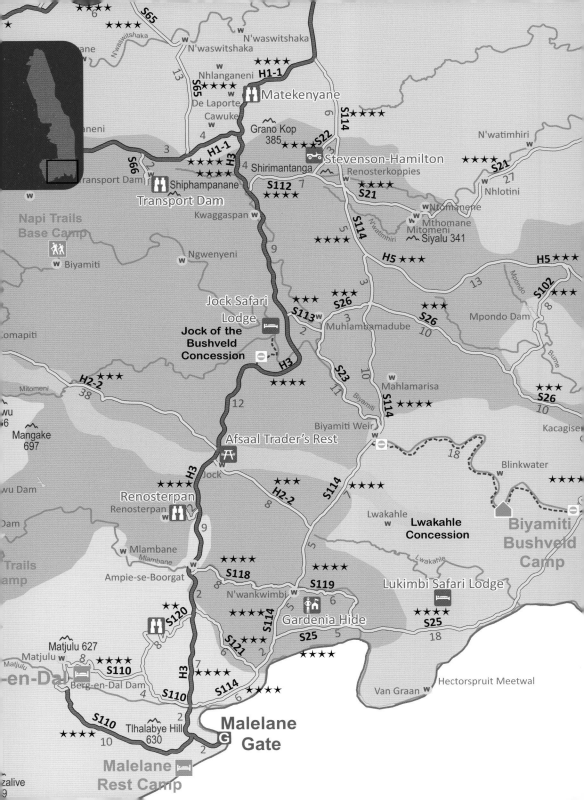

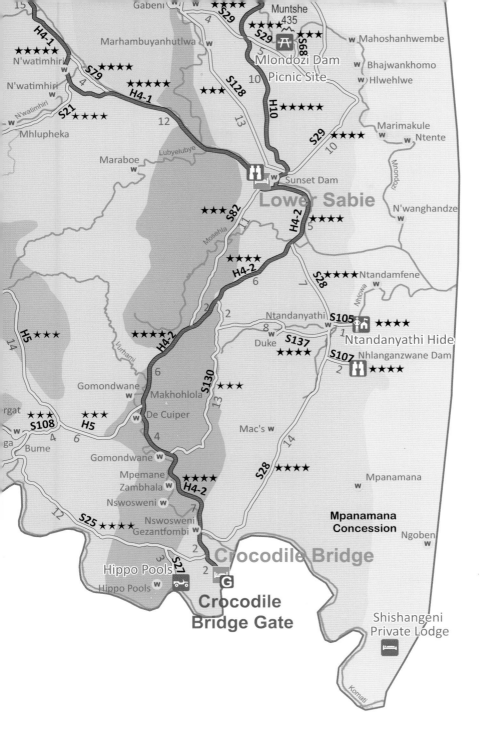

K

15

H4-1
N'watimhiri ★★★★
S79 ★★★★
N'watimhiri 4
S21 ★★★★
4
w
Mhlupheka

Gabeni w

Marhambuyanhutlwa

Maraboe w

Lubyelubye

Mosehla

Muntshe
435
S29 ★★★★
S29 ★★★★
S68 ★★★
Mahoshanhwembe w
Mlondozi Dam
Picnic Site
w Bhajwankhomo
w Hlwehlwe

H4-1 ★★★
S128

S29
10
13
H10 ★★★★★
S29 ★★★★
Marimakule
Ntente
Mnondozi

H4-2 ★★★★

Lower Sabie
Sunset Dam
w
★★★★
N'wanghandze
w

S82 ★★★
11
H4-2
5

H4-2 ★★★★
6
2
2
S28 ★★★★ Ntandamfene
7

Ntandanyathi
S105
Nhlowa

H5 ★★★
14
Ivurhami
H4-2 ★★★★
6
S130
13
Gomondwane w
Makhohlola
De Cuiper w
8
w
Duke
S137
★★★
Mac's w
S107
Ntandanyathi Hide
Nhlanganzwane Dam
★★★★
1
2
★★★★

rgat ★★★
S108
4
ga
Bume
★★★
H5
6

S28 ★★★★
14
Mpanamana
w

Gomondwane w
Mpemane
Zambhala w
Nswosweni w
S25 ★★★★
Nswosweni
Gezantfombi w
7
H4-2 ★★★★
2
Mpanamana
Concession
Ngoben

12

Crocodile Bridge
2
3
S21
Hippo Pools
Hippo Pools w
2 G
Crocodile
Bridge Gate

Shishangeni
Private Lodge
Komati

Kruger Routes

PUNDA MARIA ROUTES

- The Punda Maria area supports fewer big game species than elsewhere but offers a diversity of rare antelope species such as roan, tsessebe, eland, Sharpe's grysbok and the tiny suni antelope.
- Big herds of elephant and buffalo are often seen. A game-viewing hide overlooks a waterhole and can be reached direct from the camping area.
- The number of different bird and tree species surpasses that of any other area in the park.
- The entire north is rich in ancient history. Important archaeological sites reveal much about the early inhabitants and settlements.
- The underlying geology is fascinating and very different from the rest of the park.
- The sandveld is known as the flower garden of the park.
- The extreme north is the driest part of the park while the area around the camp is the lushest with huge trees and several springs and creeks.
- The eastern part of this area is the only place where mature mopane woodland occurs.

CLOSEST GET-OUT PLACES

- **Babalala** Picnic Site on the H1-7 – ablutions, gas braais (barbecues) for hire, cold drinks for sale, take a picnic basket.
- **Pafuri** Picnic Site on the S63 overlooking the Luvuhvu River – ablutions, gas braais for hire, cold drinks for sale, take a picnic basket. An information centre illustrates the history of the area.
- **Crooks' Corner** at the confluence of the Luvuvhu and the Limpopo Rivers – no ablutions, no picnic facilities.

PRIME DRINKING PLACES CLOSEST TO THE CAMP

- The waterhole just **outside the camp** (view from hide in the camping area).
- The natural spring at **Thulamila**.
- The natural **springs on the S99**.
- The natural **spring on the S58**.
- **Klopperfontein** Waterhole and Dam on the S61.

PRIME ROADS

- S99; S61; S58; S63; S64; H1-7; S56.

Mahonie Loop (29 km; 1 hour +) ★★★★★

H13-2; S99 circumnavigating Dimbo Hill; H13-2

Klopperfontein (62 km; 2 hours +) ★★★★

H13-2; S60; S61; Klopperfontein Waterhole and Dam; H1-8 south; H1-7 south; S58; Dzundzwini; H13-1; H13-2

Thulamila Hill (19 km; ± 1 hour) ★★★★

H13-2; H13-1; S98; Thulamila; H13-1; H13-2

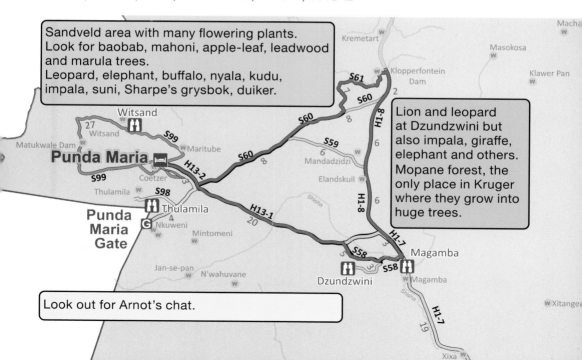

Sandveld area with many flowering plants. Look for baobab, mahoni, apple-leaf, leadwood and marula trees.
Leopard, elephant, buffalo, nyala, kudu, impala, suni, Sharpe's grysbok, duiker.

Lion and leopard at Dzundzwini but also impala, giraffe, elephant and others. Mopane forest, the only place in Kruger where they grow into huge trees.

Look out for Arnot's chat.

Shingwedzi (151 km; 6 hours)

H13-2; H13-1; H1-7 south; Babalala; S56; H1-7 south; Shingwedzi; H1-7 north; H13-1; H13-2

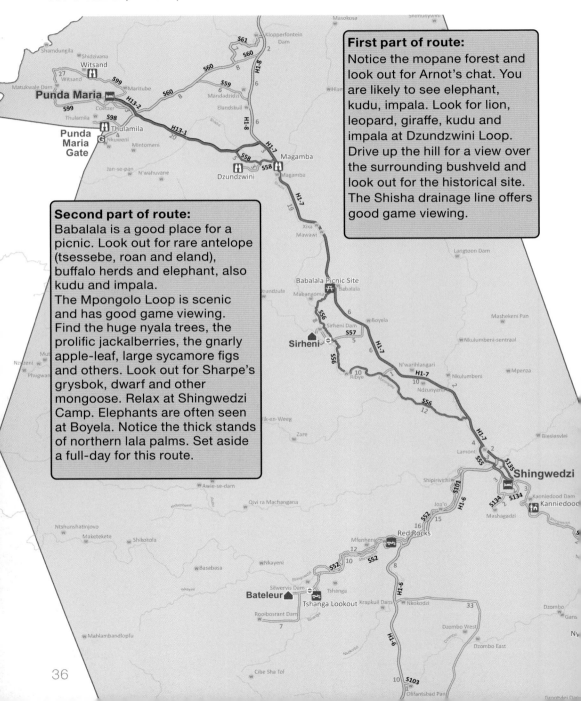

First part of route:
Notice the mopane forest and look out for Arnot's chat. You are likely to see elephant, kudu, impala. Look for lion, leopard, giraffe, kudu and impala at Dzundzwini Loop. Drive up the hill for a view over the surrounding bushveld and look out for the historical site. The Shisha drainage line offers good game viewing.

Second part of route:
Babalala is a good place for a picnic. Look out for rare antelope (tsessebe, roan and eland), buffalo herds and elephant, also kudu and impala.
The Mpongolo Loop is scenic and has good game viewing. Find the huge nyala trees, the prolific jackalberries, the gnarly apple-leaf, large sycamore figs and others. Look out for Sharpe's grysbok, dwarf and other mongoose. Relax at Shingwedzi Camp. Elephants are often seen at Boyela. Notice the thick stands of northern lala palms. Set aside a full-day for this route.

Pafuri (132 km; 5.5 hours) ★★★★★

H13-2; S60; S61; H1-8 north; S64; S63; Pafuri Picnic Site; S63; H1-8; H13-1; H13-2

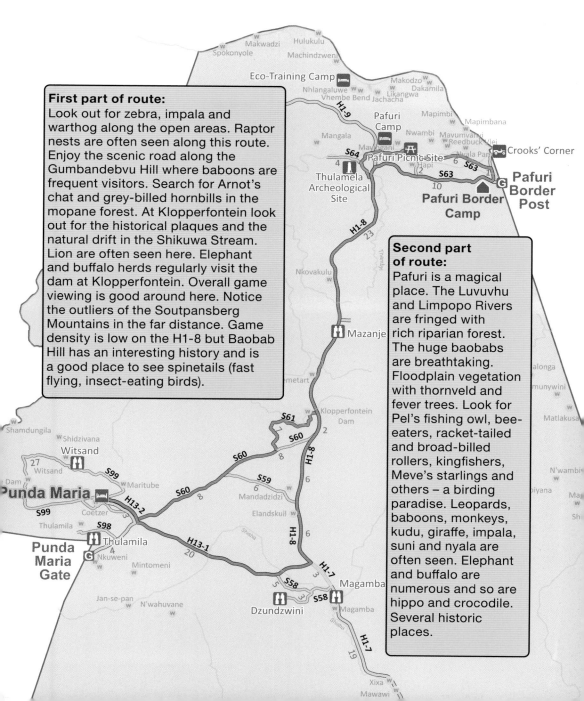

First part of route:
Look out for zebra, impala and warthog along the open areas. Raptor nests are often seen along this route. Enjoy the scenic road along the Gumbandebvu Hill where baboons are frequent visitors. Search for Arnot's chat and grey-billed hornbills in the mopane forest. At Klopperfontein look out for the historical plaques and the natural drift in the Shikuwa Stream. Lion are often seen here. Elephant and buffalo herds regularly visit the dam at Klopperfontein. Overall game viewing is good around here. Notice the outliers of the Soutpansberg Mountains in the far distance. Game density is low on the H1-8 but Baobab Hill has an interesting history and is a good place to see spinetails (fast flying, insect-eating birds).

Second part of route:
Pafuri is a magical place. The Luvuvhu and Limpopo Rivers are fringed with rich riparian forest. The huge baobabs are breathtaking. Floodplain vegetation with thornveld and fever trees. Look for Pel's fishing owl, bee-eaters, racket-tailed and broad-billed rollers, kingfishers, Meve's starlings and others – a birding paradise. Leopards, baboons, monkeys, kudu, giraffe, impala, suni and nyala are often seen. Elephant and buffalo are numerous and so are hippo and crocodile. Several historic places.

SHINGWEDZI ROUTES

- In mopane veld the best game viewing is along the rivers. The best time for seeing game is in the dry months when the seasonal rivers recede and competition for diminishing water resources is at its peak.
- This is elephant country and huge breeding herds of 50–60 of the largest land mammals in the world congregate at water points.
- The Shingwedzi area was home to the famous Magnificent Seven tuskers. All have now died and their stories and ivory can be viewed at the Letaba Camp.
- Buffalo do well around Shingwedzi and they often come down in their hundreds to drink.
- The Kanniedood Dam was built in 1975 and created a permanent water supply for about 21 km downstream from the camp. In the 2013 floods, the dam wall was broken and this changed the entire nature of the previously popular Kanniedood Drive. Many pools remain but their positions have changed.
- Gold prospecting at Red Rocks in the early 19th century forms part of the history of the magnificent Shingwedzi River. Fortunately not much of the precious metal was found, and nature was allowed to rest in peace.

CLOSEST GET-OUT PLACES
- **Babalala** Picnic Site – ablutions, gas braais for hire, cold drinks for sale, take a picnic basket.
- **Tshanga** Lookout – no picnic facilities except rustic tables and bush toilets.
- **Nyawutsi** Hide on the S50 – no ablutions, no picnic facilities.

PRIME DRINKING PLACES CLOSEST TO THE CAMP
- Several **pools** in the Shingwedzi and Mphongolo Rivers.
- The **Lamont** Waterhole on S55.
- **Causeway** across the river below the camp.

PRIME ROADS

- H1-7; river drive on northern section of the S50; S56; S52; first southern section of the H1-6.

Confluence (8 km; 0.5 hours) ★★★★

H1-6 to confluence

Tshanga (66 km; ± 3 hours) ★★★★

H1-6; S52; Tshanga Lookout; S52 east; H1-6 north

Grootvlei Dam via Kanniedood (76 km; ± 3 hours) ★★★★

S50; Dipeni; S50; S54 Nyawutsi Bird Hide; Grootvlei Dam; back on the S50

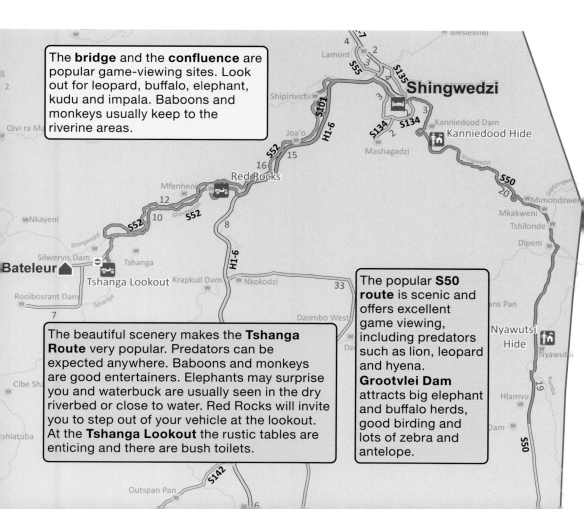

The **bridge** and the **confluence** are popular game-viewing sites. Look out for leopard, buffalo, elephant, kudu and impala. Baboons and monkeys usually keep to the riverine areas.

The beautiful scenery makes the **Tshanga Route** very popular. Predators can be expected anywhere. Baboons and monkeys are good entertainers. Elephants may surprise you and waterbuck are usually seen in the dry riverbed or close to water. Red Rocks will invite you to step out of your vehicle at the lookout. At the **Tshanga Lookout** the rustic tables are enticing and there are bush toilets.

The popular **S50 route** is scenic and offers excellent game viewing, including predators such as lion, leopard and hyena. **Grootvlei Dam** attracts big elephant and buffalo herds, good birding and lots of zebra and antelope.

Pafuri (212 km; 8.5 hours) ★★★★

H1-7; Babalala; H1-7; H1-8 north; S64; S63; Pafuri Picnic Site; S63; H1-8; H1-7; S135

Babalala (71 km; ± 3 hours) ★★★★★

H1-7; S56; Babalala; H1-7 south; S135

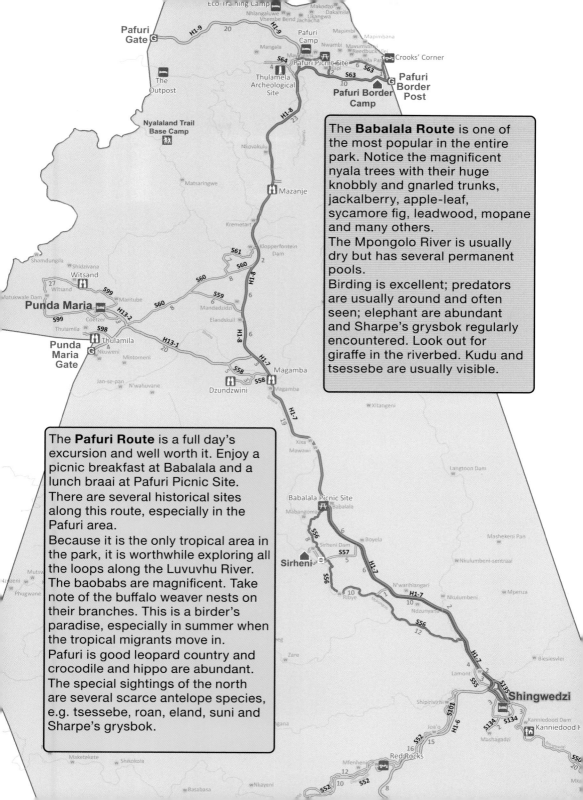

The **Babalala Route** is one of the most popular in the entire park. Notice the magnificent nyala trees with their huge knobbly and gnarled trunks, jackalberry, apple-leaf, sycamore fig, leadwood, mopane and many others.
The Mpongolo River is usually dry but has several permanent pools.
Birding is excellent; predators are usually around and often seen; elephant are abundant and Sharpe's grysbok regularly encountered. Look out for giraffe in the riverbed. Kudu and tsessebe are usually visible.

The **Pafuri Route** is a full day's excursion and well worth it. Enjoy a picnic breakfast at Babalala and a lunch braai at Pafuri Picnic Site.
There are several historical sites along this route, especially in the Pafuri area.
Because it is the only tropical area in the park, it is worthwhile exploring all the loops along the Luvuvhu River. The baobabs are magnificent. Take note of the buffalo weaver nests on their branches. This is a birder's paradise, especially in summer when the tropical migrants move in.
Pafuri is good leopard country and crocodile and hippo are abundant.
The special sightings of the north are several scarce antelope species, e.g. tsessebe, roan, eland, suni and Sharpe's grysbok.

MOPANI ROUTES

- The camp is situated in mopane shrubveld with underlying basalt rock but the proximity to the seasonal Shipandani and Tsendze rivers means there is riverine vegetation and therefore a greater diversity of tree species.
- The grass is sweet towards the surrounding eastern plains and attracts more game than the areas to the west (S142 and S146).
- Although game is less abundant on the western roads, the landscape becomes stunning after rains. Pans fill up and water lilies with their delicate-hued flowers appear from nowhere. Silver clusterleaf is prolific and gives a soft tone to areas where there are seepage lines.
- To the east, the Nshawu drainage line – with wetland areas and pans – is the main attraction, while animals of different kinds are always present at Mooiplaas Waterhole. If you don't see animals it may be because there are predators nearby.
- The Tropic of Capricorn Road is a magical sight when huge tuskers approach the waterhole from all directions.

CLOSEST GET-OUT PLACES

- **Mooiplaas** Picnic Site – shaded lookout platform, ablutions, gas braais for hire, cold drinks for sale, take a picnic basket.
- **Shibavantsengele** Lookout – no ablutions, no picnic facilities.
- **Makhadzi** Picnic Site – ablutions, gas braais for hire, cold drinks for sale, take a picnic basket.
- **Shipandani** Overnight Hide – ablutions for overnight guests.
- **Pioneer** Viewing Hide – no ablutions, no picnic facilities.

PRIME DRINKING PLACES CLOSEST TO THE CAMP

- **Pioneer Dam** views from the camp.
- **Mooiplaas** Waterhole.
- **Bowkerskop**.
- **Nshawu** Wetlands (seasonal).

PRIME ROADS

- S50; S49; the southern end of S142; H1-6 up to Middelvlei.

Shipandani Hide and Mooiplaas (33 km; ± 1.5 hours) ★★★★★

H1-6 south; S142 west; Shipandani; S142 east; H1-6; S49; Mooiplaas Waterhole; S49; S50 south; H1-6 north; Mooiplaas Picnic Site; H1-6 north

Makhadzi Picnic Site (83km; ± 3.3 hours) ★★★

H1-6 south; Tsendze Loops; H1-6 south; Mooiplaas Picnic Site; S48; H15; Makhadzi; H15 west; H1-6 north

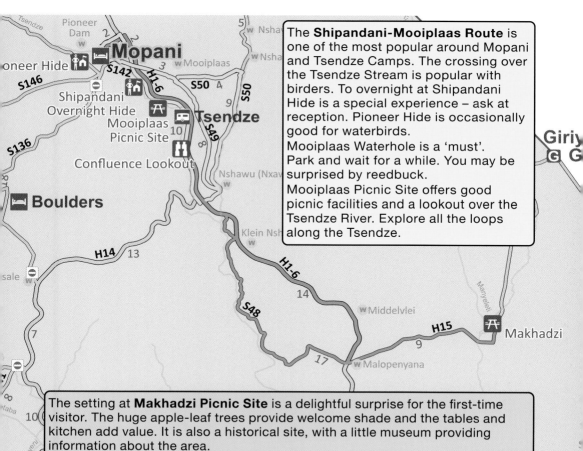

The **Shipandani-Mooiplaas Route** is one of the most popular around Mopani and Tsendze Camps. The crossing over the Tsendze Stream is popular with birders. To overnight at Shipandani Hide is a special experience – ask at reception. Pioneer Hide is occasionally good for waterbirds.
Mooiplaas Waterhole is a 'must'. Park and wait for a while. You may be surprised by reedbuck.
Mooiplaas Picnic Site offers good picnic facilities and a lookout over the Tsendze River. Explore all the loops along the Tsendze.

The setting at **Makhadzi Picnic Site** is a delightful surprise for the first-time visitor. The huge apple-leaf trees provide welcome shade and the tables and kitchen add value. It is also a historical site, with a little museum providing information about the area.
Game densities along this route are low but zebra and impala are usually seen. The S48 meanders along the Tsendze although pools are usually dry. Predators are scarce except for hyena which are occasionally encountered.

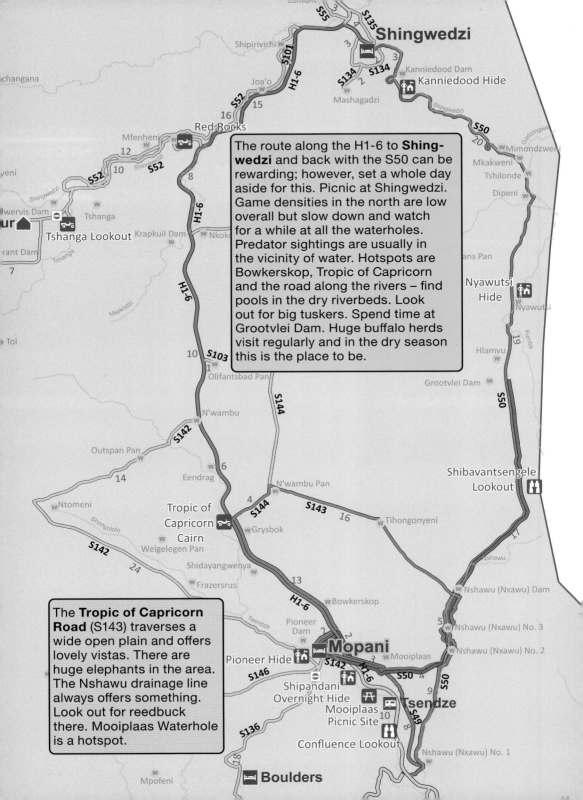

Shingwedzi

Kanniedood Dam
Kanniedood Hide

Mashagadzi

Red Rocks

Mfenheni

Tshanga Lookout   Krapkuil Dam

Nkoko

Mimondzweni

Mkakweni
Tshilonde

Dipeni

Nyawutsi
Hide
Nyawutsi

The route along the H1-6 to **Shing-wedzi** and back with the S50 can be rewarding; however, set a whole day aside for this. Picnic at Shingwedzi. Game densities in the north are low overall but slow down and watch for a while at all the waterholes. Predator sightings are usually in the vicinity of water. Hotspots are Bowkerskop, Tropic of Capricorn and the road along the rivers – find pools in the dry riverbeds. Look out for big tuskers. Spend time at Grootvlei Dam. Huge buffalo herds visit regularly and in the dry season this is the place to be.

Olifantsbad Pan

N'wambu

Grootvlei Dam

Hlamvu

Outspan Pan

Eendrag

N'wambu Pan

Shibavantsengele
Lookout

Ntomeni

Tropic of
Capricorn
Cairn
Welgelegen Pan

Grysbok

Tihongonyeni

Shidayangwenya

Frazersrus

Bowkerskop

Nshawu (Nxawu) Dam

Nshawu (Nxawu) No. 3

The **Tropic of Capricorn Road** (S143) traverses a wide open plain and offers lovely vistas. There are huge elephants in the area. The Nshawu drainage line always offers something. Look out for reedbuck there. Mooiplaas Waterhole is a hotspot.

Pioneer
Dam

Mopani

Mooiplaas

Nshawu (Nxawu) No. 2

Pioneer Hide

Shipandani
Overnight Hide
Mooiplaas
Picnic Site

Tsendze

Confluence Lookout

Nshawu (Nxawu) No. 1

Boulders

Mpofeni

Shingwedzi Camp (131 km; ± 8.5 hours) ★★★★

H1-6 south; S50; Grootvlei Dam; S50 north; Dipeni; S50 (Kanniedood Dam Road); Shingwedzi; H1-6 south

Grootvlei Dam via Nshawu (68 km; ± 3 hours) ★★★★

H1-6 south; S50; Nshawu; Shibavantsengele; S50 north up to Grootvlei Dam; back via S50; H1-6 north

Tropic of Capricorn Road (51 km; ± 2 hours) ★★★

H1-6 south; S49; S50; S143 – Tropic of Capricorn Road; S144 south; H1-6 south

LETABA ROUTES

- Letaba and elephants are synonymous. These giants need to drink regularly and are prolific near the river.
- The riverine vegetation in the camp and along the river banks offers good birding opportunities.
- Away from the river, the mopane shrubveld on basalt offers mostly sweet grass, although it is sparse.
- Towards Phalaborwa, mopane and bushwillow woodlands are prevalent and game densities are relatively low.
- The area is rich in prehistorical sites. Archeological excavations reveal a fascinating story of Stone Age people who were gradually displaced by other tribes who mined copper and iron and traded with Arabs and others. The Masorini Site on the H9 is worth visiting.

CLOSEST GET-OUT PLACES
- **Matambeni Bird Hide** on S62 – no ablutions, no picnic facilities.
- **Makhadzi** on H15 – ablutions, gas braais for hire, cold drinks for sale, take a picnic basket.
- **Mooiplaas** on H1-6 – ablutions, gas braais for hire, cold drinks for sale, take a picnic basket.
- **Masorini** on H9 – ablutions, gas braais for hire, cold drinks for sale, take a picnic basket.
- **N'wamanzi** Lookout – no ablutions, no picnic facilities.

PRIME DRINKING PLACES CLOSEST TO THE CAMP
- The **Letaba River** north and east of the camp.
- **Nhlanganini Dam** on the H9.
- **Engelhard Dam** on the S62.

PRIME ROADS
- Southern end of H1-6; S95; S62; S46; S69.

Masorini and Phalaborwa Gate (100 km; ± 4 hours)   ★★★

H9; S69; S70; H9; Masorini; H9; gate and back via S131; H9

Mingerhout Dam (38 km; 1.5 hours)   ★★★

H1-6 north; river frontage; S95; S47; Mingerhout Dam; S47 south; S131; H9

Olifants Camp (70 km; ± 3 hours)   ★★★

S46; river frontage; S93; S44; lookout; S44; Olifants Camp; H8; N'wamanzi Lookout; H1-5 north

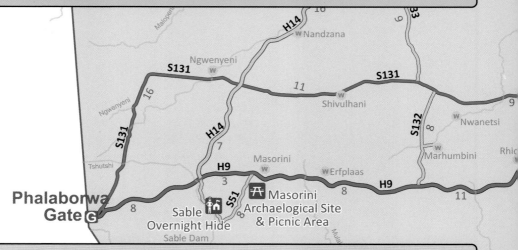

The **Masorini Route** to Phalaborwa Gate is rewarding at times despite the low density of game in mopane veld. The Nhlanganini Loop is scenic. Expect elephant and buffalo, browsing antelope and giraffe, zebra and wildebeest. Spend time at the Nhlanganini Dam. Lion and leopard usually keep close to water. Wild dog are often seen on this route. Visit Sable Dam.
The hotspot is the Masorini Historical Site that provides an insight into 16th century ironmakers and traders. There are klipspringer on the koppies. Look out for the rare sable. S131: game concentrated at waterholes.

The route to **Olifants Camp** traverses mopane shrubveld with mainly sweet grasses. The banks of the Letaba River may yield lion and leopard sightings. Zebra, wildebeest, impala and the odd duiker and kudu can be expected. Look out for the Von Wiellich's Baobab on the S93. The lookouts over the Olifants River are hotspots. Notice the change in vegetation as you climb the hills. Hippo and crocodile are abundant in the two rivers. Baboons and monkeys occur in riverine vegetation. Picnic at Olifants Camp.

Mingerhout (Matumi) Loop is particularly scenic. Notice the gnarled apple-leaf trees on the banks of the Letaba. Look out for lion and leopard close to water. Baboons and monkeys abound. Elephant, kudu and impala as well as bushbuck and nyala are frequently visible.

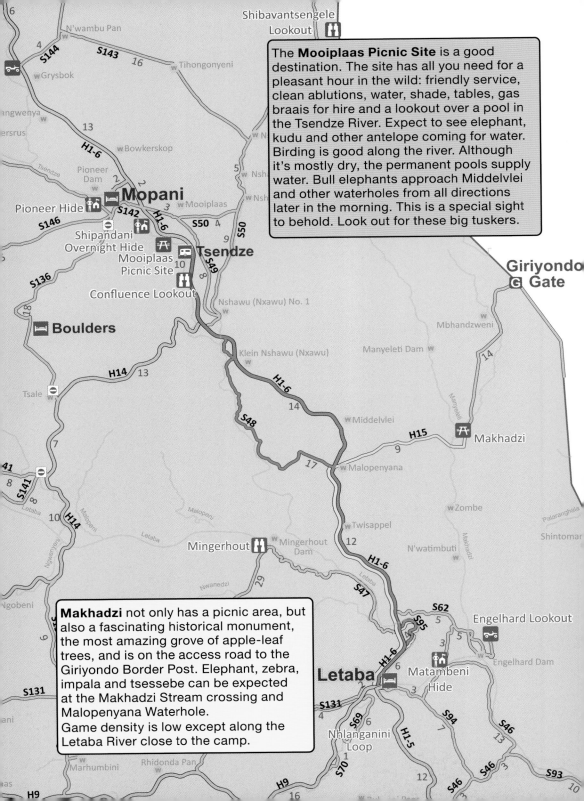

Shibavantsengele
Lookout

The **Mooiplaas Picnic Site** is a good
destination. The site has all you need for a
pleasant hour in the wild: friendly service,
clean ablutions, water, shade, tables, gas
braais for hire and a lookout over a pool in
the Tsendze River. Expect to see elephant,
kudu and other antelope coming for water.
Birding is good along the river. Although
it's mostly dry, the permanent pools supply
water. Bull elephants approach Middelvlei
and other waterholes from all directions
later in the morning. This is a special sight
to behold. Look out for these big tuskers.

N'wambu Pan

Tihongonyeni

4
S144

S143   16

Grysbok

angwenya

ersrus

13

H1-6

Bowkerskop

Tsendze

5

Pioneer
Dam   2

Nsh

Mooiplaas   3   Nsh

Pioneer Hide

Mopani

S142   H1-6

S146

S50   4   S50

9

Shipandani
Overnight Hide

Tsendze

S49

Mooiplaas
Picnic Site

10

8

**Giriyondo
G Gate**

S136

Confluence Lookout

Nshawu (Nxawu) No. 1

Mbhandzweni

18

Boulders

Klein Nshawu (Nxawu)

Manyeleti Dam

14

H14   13

H1-6

Tsale

S48   14

Manyeleti

Middelvlei

H15

Makhadzi

7

17   Malopenyana   9

41

8   S141

Zombe

Palaranghala

10   H14

Malopeni

Letaba

Malopeni

Twisappel

N'watimbuti

Shintomar

Mingerhout   Mingerhout
Dam

12

H1-6

Nwanedzi   29

S47

Makhadzi not only has a picnic area, but
also a fascinating historical monument,
the most amazing grove of apple-leaf
trees, and is on the access road to the
Giriyondo Border Post. Elephant, zebra,
impala and tsessebe can be expected
at the Makhadzi Stream crossing and
Malopenyana Waterhole.
Game density is low except along the
Letaba River close to the camp.

Ngobeni

S62

Engelhard Lookout

S95   5

S131

H1-6   3   5   Engelhard Dam

Matambeni
Hide

Letaba   6

3

S131   S69   6

S94   S46

4

Nhlanganini
Loop

S70   H1-5   13

Marhumbini   Rhidonda Pan

12   S46   3   S93

H9   H9   16

Mooiplaas Picnic Site (74 km; ± 3 hours) ★★★

H1-6 north; river frontage; S95; H1-6; Mooiplaas; H1-6 south; S48; H1-6 south

Makhadzi Picnic Site (64 km; ± 2.5 hours) ★★★

H1-6 north; river frontage; S95; H1-6; H15; Makhadzi; H15 west; H1-6

Letaba River Bridge (13.6 km; ± 1 hour) ★★★★★

H1-6 north; river frontage; S95; bridge over Letaba; turn back on H1-6 south

Engelhard Dam to Lookout (60 km; 2 hours) ★★★★★

H1-6 north; river frontage; S95; bridge; H1-6 north; S62; lookout; S62; H1-6 south

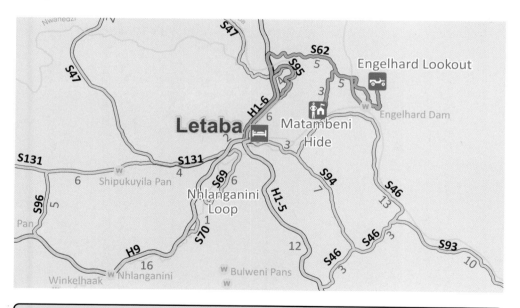

Early mornings and late afternoons are favourite times along the **Letaba Bridge Route** and the **Engelhard Dam Route**. It is along the Letaba River and across the wide riverbed with occasional deep pools where everything happens. Predators such as lion, leopard and hyena are regularly seen. So are baboons and monkeys, mongoose and genet (late afternoon and on night drives), elephant, hippo and crocodile, kudu, waterbuck and impala – even zebra and wildebeest. The Matambeni Hide is not as active since the water has receded, but all the other loops towards the Engelhard Lookout are worth doing. A historical site at the end of one of the loops is of interest.

OLIFANTS CAMP ROUTES

- The Olifants River area is in the transition zone between the southern thornveld, wooded savanna and the northern mopane veld.
- Game density is lower than in the south but diversity is great.
- Mopane bush is dense and visibility generally not good.
- Browsers do better than grazers in this area.
- The best game drive routes are those following river courses.
- It is prime elephant territory.
- The Olifants River is home to the largest crocodile population in the park.

CLOSEST GET-OUT PLACES

- **N'wamanzi Lookout** – no ablutions, no picnic facilities.
- **Olifants Lookout** – no ablutions, no picnic facilities.
- **Letaba Rest Camp** – full-house amenities.
- **Timbavati Picnic Site** – ablutions, gas braais for hire, cold drinks for sale, take a picnic basket.
- The causeway over the Olifants River to Balule on the S92.
- Any of the river viewing spots.

PRIME DRINKING PLACES CLOSEST TO THE CAMP

- After good rains, the **pan at the S93 and S44** fills up and offers good sunset viewing close to the camp.
- The bridge crossing over the **Olifants River on the H1-5**.

PRIME ROADS

- S92; S91; S90; S44; S93; S89; S39.

Olifants Lookout and Lower Letaba (52 km; ± 2 hours) ★★★

S44; view site; S93; S46; Letaba River frontage; Letaba; H1-5 south; H8

Letaba Camp (78 km; ± 3 hours) ★★★

S93; S46 along river; Letaba Camp; H1-6; S95 up to bridge; back on the H1-6; H1-5; H8

Ngotso (48 km; ± 2 hours) ★★★★★

H8; H1-5; H1-4; S147 (new one-way road); S89; S90; S92; H8

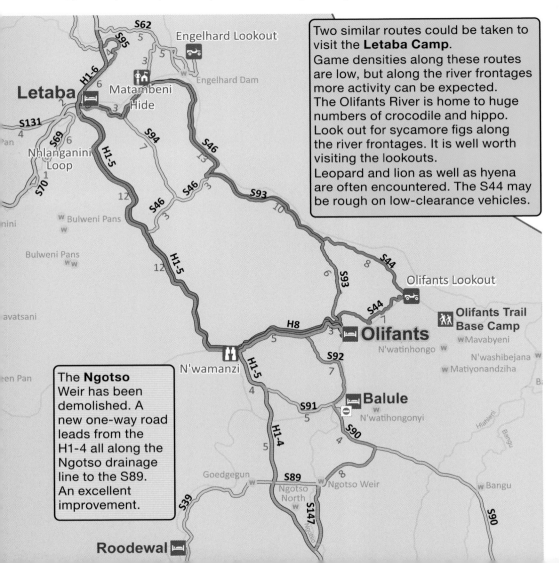

Two similar routes could be taken to visit the **Letaba Camp**.
Game densities along these routes are low, but along the river frontages more activity can be expected.
The Olifants River is home to huge numbers of crocodile and hippo.
Look out for sycamore figs along the river frontages. It is well worth visiting the lookouts.
Leopard and lion as well as hyena are often encountered. The S44 may be rough on low-clearance vehicles.

The **Ngotso** Weir has been demolished. A new one-way road leads from the H1-4 all along the Ngotso drainage line to the S89. An excellent improvement.

Satara via S100 (126 km; ± 5 hours) ★★★★

H8; S92; S90; S41; S100; Satara; H1-4; H1-5; H8

Timbavati Picnic Site (132 km; ± 5.5 hours) ★★★★

H8; S92; S90; S89; S39; Timbavati Picnic Site; S40; H7; Satara; H1-4; S147; S89; H1-4; H1-5; H8

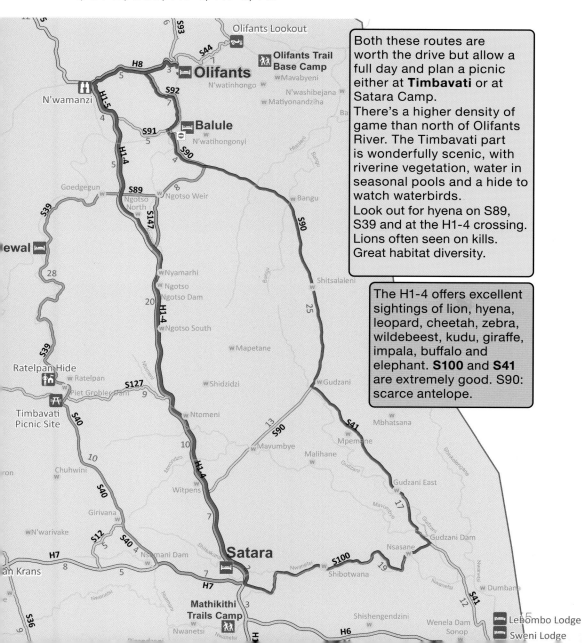

Both these routes are worth the drive but allow a full day and plan a picnic either at **Timbavati** or at Satara Camp.

There's a higher density of game than north of Olifants River. The Timbavati part is wonderfully scenic, with riverine vegetation, water in seasonal pools and a hide to watch waterbirds.

Look out for hyena on S89, S39 and at the H1-4 crossing. Lions often seen on kills. Great habitat diversity.

The H1-4 offers excellent sightings of lion, hyena, leopard, cheetah, zebra, wildebeest, kudu, giraffe, impala, buffalo and elephant. **S100** and **S41** are extremely good. S90: scarce antelope.

SATARA ROUTES

- To the west is a strip of Ecca shale with sweet grazing, while the soils in the far west have underlying granite and gabbro, and grasses tend to become unpalatable in winter.
- The frequency of lion sightings is extremely high around Satara.
- Game is prolific on most of the routes radiating from Satara.
- The grassy plains surrounding Satara are referred to as the fertile central plains.
- To the east of Satara are the basalt plains with sweet grazing, fringed by the Lebombo Mountains on the border of Mozambique.

CLOSEST GET-OUT PLACES

- **N'wanetsi Picnic Site** on the H6 – shaded lookout platform, ablutions, gas braais for hire, cold drinks for sale, take a picnic basket.
- **Tshokwane Picnic Site** on the H1-3 – ablutions, small shop, gas braais for hire, take a picnic basket or buy basic food items or meals.
- **Muzandzeni Picnic Site** on the S36 – ablutions, gas braais for hire, cold drinks for sale, take a picnic basket.
- **Timbavati Picnic Site** on the S40 – ablutions, gas braais for hire, cold drinks for sale, take a picnic basket.
- **Sweni Bird Hide** on the S37 – no ablutions.
- **Nhlanguleni Picnic Site** on the S36 – ablutions, gas braais for hire, cold drinks for sale, take a picnic basket.
- **Ratelpan Hide** on the S39 – no ablutions.

PRIME DRINKING PLACES CLOSEST TO THE CAMP

- **N'wanetsi Dam** on the H6.
- **Nsemani Dam** on the N7.
- **Girivana Dam** on the S12.
- **Kumana Dam** on the H1-3.
- **Orpen Dam** on the S32.
- **Gudzani Dam** on the S41.

PRIME ROADS

- H7; H1-3; S100; S41; H6; S90; S39; S126.

Tshokwane Picnic Site (110 km; ± 4.5 hours) ★★★★★

H1-3; Tshokwane Picnic Site; optional loop to Orpen Dam (S32; S35); back via S34; S36; S125; H1-3

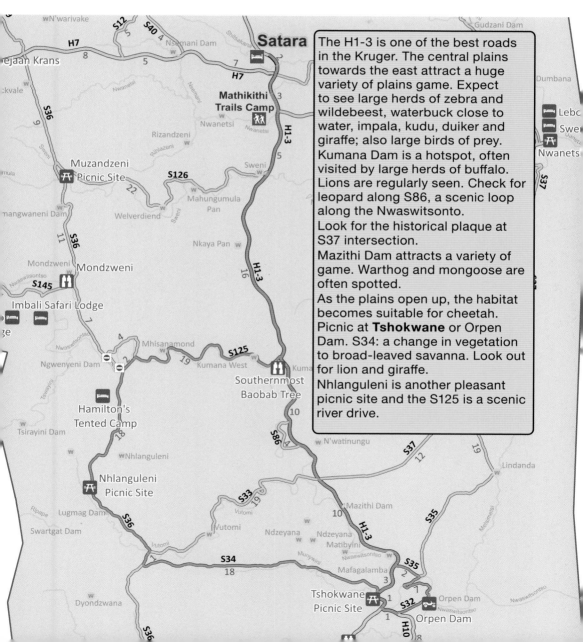

The H1-3 is one of the best roads in the Kruger. The central plains towards the east attract a huge variety of plains game. Expect to see large herds of zebra and wildebeest, waterbuck close to water, impala, kudu, duiker and giraffe; also large birds of prey. Kumana Dam is a hotspot, often visited by large herds of buffalo. Lions are regularly seen. Check for leopard along S86, a scenic loop along the Nwaswitsonto.

Look for the historical plaque at S37 intersection.

Mazithi Dam attracts a variety of game. Warthog and mongoose are often spotted.

As the plains open up, the habitat becomes suitable for cheetah.

Picnic at **Tshokwane** or Orpen Dam. S34: a change in vegetation to broad-leaved savanna. Look out for lion and giraffe.

Nhlanguleni is another pleasant picnic site and the S125 is a scenic river drive.

Orpen Gate (117 km; ± 5 hours) ★★★★

H1-3; H7; back via S106

Muzandzeni Picnic Site (74 km; ± 3 hours) ★★★★

H1-3; S126, Muzandzeni Picnic Site; S36 north; H7; back via H1-3

The **Orpen** drive can be surprisingly productive. The H7 at the Satara end is ideal habitat for cheetah. Notice the many mature marula trees along the way. Scan the branches for leopard. Lion are also active in this area. Nsemani Dam is a hotspot for game. Spend some time on the dam wall part of the road to watch what the animals are doing. Use binoculars to scan the bushes for approaching game. The road over the Nsemani Dam wall and beyond traverses Delagoa thornveld, which is particularly popular with game. Expect to see many kudu, giraffe, impala, zebra, blue wildebeest and elephant along this stretch. Many lion and leopard sightings are reported here. Once at Bobbejaan Krans, scan the dry riverbed of the Timbavati for elephant. The riverine vegetation is a delight as you continue along the Timbavati. Watch out for leopard.

The vegetation on S106 is totally different. Look out for bustards along this road.

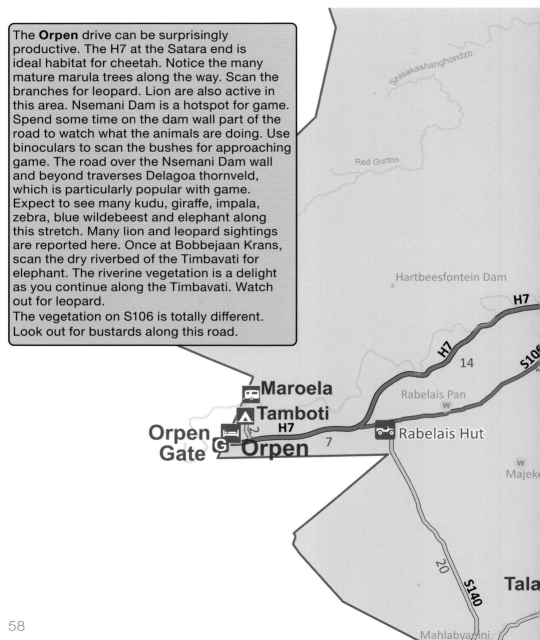

Nsemani Dam (32 km; ± 1.5 hours) ★★★★★

H1-3; H7; Nsemani Dam; S12 to Girivana Dam, back to H7 via S40; H7 then onto H1-3 back to camp

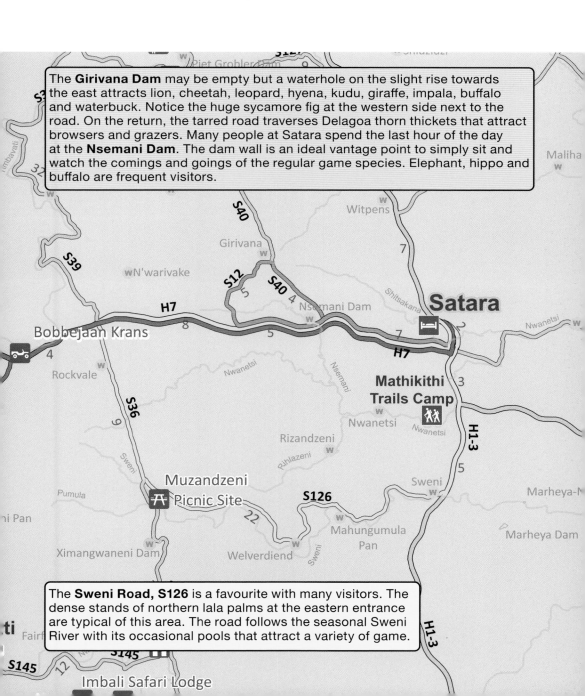

The **Girivana Dam** may be empty but a waterhole on the slight rise towards the east attracts lion, cheetah, leopard, hyena, kudu, giraffe, impala, buffalo and waterbuck. Notice the huge sycamore fig at the western side next to the road. On the return, the tarred road traverses Delagoa thorn thickets that attract browsers and grazers. Many people at Satara spend the last hour of the day at the **Nsemani Dam**. The dam wall is an ideal vantage point to simply sit and watch the comings and goings of the regular game species. Elephant, hippo and buffalo are frequent visitors.

The **Sweni Road, S126** is a favourite with many visitors. The dense stands of northern lala palms at the eastern entrance are typical of this area. The road follows the seasonal Sweni River with its occasional pools that attract a variety of game.

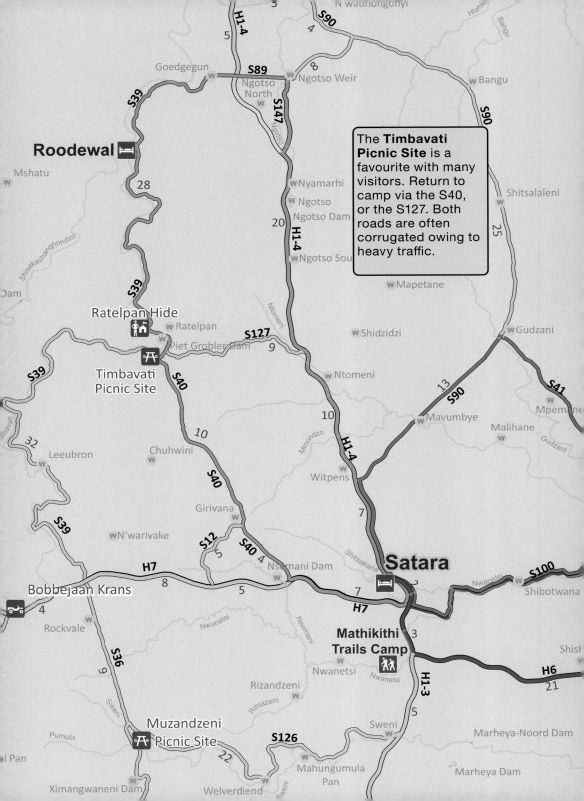

The **Timbavati Picnic Site** is a favourite with many visitors. Return to camp via the S40, or the S127. Both roads are often corrugated owing to heavy traffic.

Upper Timbavati River (91 km; ± 4 hours) ★★★★

H1-4 north; S147; S89; S39; Timbavati Picnic Site; S40; H7; H1-3

N'wanetsi Picnic Site (90 km; ± 4 hours) ★★★★★

H1-4 north; S90; S41; N'wanetsi Picnic Site; H6; S37 to Sweni Hide over the Sweni River and back on H6 east via S41 and S100 or via H6 back to camp

Gudzani Dam (58 km; ± 2 hours) ★★★★

H1-3; S100; Gudzani Dam; S41 to N'wanetsi Picnic Site, back via H6 and H1-3

The **Timbavati Route** is magical. The H1-4 up to the S89 intersection is the recommended start. The first stretch of the tar road is good for cheetah. Slightly further on is good for lion. Look out for buffalo and elephant. The S127 usually has a poor surface and is therefore not recommended. Enter the Timbavati meander from the north. Notice the beginning of mopane vegetation northwards. The Timbavati flows into the Olifants River. Although the Timbavati is seasonal, several pools along its course provide water during the dry season. Lush riverine vegetation fringes the river course and is ideal habitat for leopard. Browsers are abundant and grazers move into the riverbed in search of water. Lion and hyena can be expected. Baboons and monkeys keep close to the river. The Ratelpan Hide and Grobler Dam are popular.

The route to **N'wanetsi Picnic Site** passes Gudzani Dam and continues to N'wanetsi and the Sweni Hide hotspot. This is prime lion country but hyena, cheetah and leopard can also be spotted. Jackal are found all over the park and are always ready to take advantage of a kill. Honey badgers are seen on this route from time to time, as are swarms of red-billed quelea at certain times of the year. The Sweni Hide is ideal for spending time just watching the surroundings. The N'wanetsi Picnic Site has ablutions, gas braais for hire, shaded seating and a lookout on the hill. The S100 is usually a winner.

The **S100, S41 and H6 triangle** is known as one of the best for predator sightings in the park. Surprisingly, there are more leopard than lion in the park. Although both are generally nocturnal, they are regularly seen during the daytime. This triangle is rich in plains game, buffalo and elephant. Birding is excellent.

Gudzani East

Gudzani Dam

Nwanetsi

Dumbana

Wenela Dam

Sonop

🛏 Lebombo Lodge

🛏 Sweni Lodge

🍴 Nwanetsi Picnic Site

Nwanetsi Dam

Sweni Hide

🚶 Sweni Trails
Base Camp

ORPEN, TAMBOTI AND MAROELA ROUTES

- The sweet grass in the vicinity of the camps attracts many grazers.
- This in turn attracts cheetah, lion and leopard.
- Wild dog are also seen from time to time.
- A small waterhole outside the Orpen Camp fence offers game viewing throughout the day.
- The seasonal Timbavati River and the riverine vegetation offer great game viewing from the Tamboti and Maroela Camps.

CLOSEST GET-OUT PLACES

- **N'wanetsi Picnic Site** on the H6 – shaded lookout platform, ablutions, gas braais for hire, cold drinks for sale, take a picnic basket.
- **Tshokwane Picnic Site** on the H1-3 – ablutions, small shop, gas braais for hire, take a picnic basket or buy basic food items or meals.
- **Muzandzeni Picnic Site** on the S36 – ablutions, gas braais for hire, cold drinks for sale, take a picnic basket.
- **Timbavati Picnic Site** on the S40 – ablutions, gas braais for hire, cold drinks for sale, take a picnic basket.
- **Sweni Bird Hide** on the S37 – no ablutions.
- **Nhlanguleni Picnic Site** on the S36 – ablutions, gas braais for hire, cold drinks for sale, take a picnic basket.
- **Ratelpan Hide** on the S39 – no ablutions.

PRIME DRINKING PLACES CLOSEST TO THE CAMP

- **Nsemani Dam** on the H7.
- **Girivana Dam** on the S12.

PRIME ROADS

- S41; S39; H7; H1-4; H1-3; S100; S126; southern section of S90.

Upper Timbavati (133 km; ± 5.5 hours) ★★★★

H7; S39; Timbavati Picnic Site; S39; Roodewal; S39; back on the H1-4 and H7

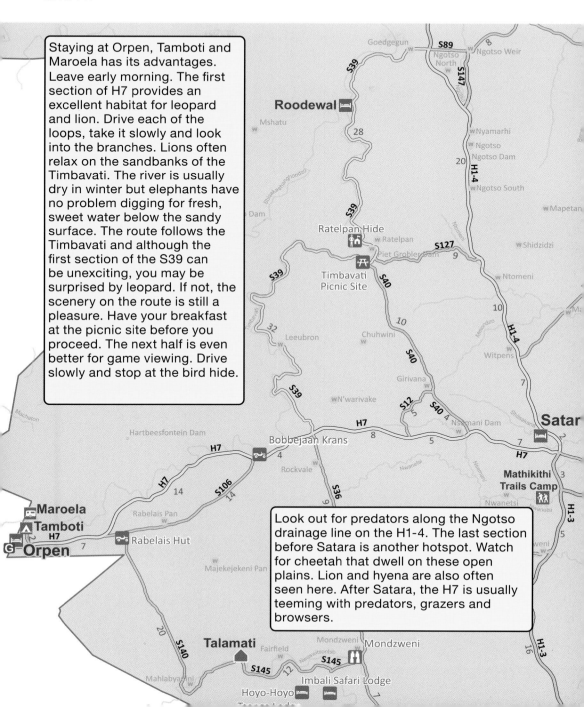

Staying at Orpen, Tamboti and Maroela has its advantages. Leave early morning. The first section of H7 provides an excellent habitat for leopard and lion. Drive each of the loops, take it slowly and look into the branches. Lions often relax on the sandbanks of the Timbavati. The river is usually dry in winter but elephants have no problem digging for fresh, sweet water below the sandy surface. The route follows the Timbavati and although the first section of the S39 can be unexciting, you may be surprised by leopard. If not, the scenery on the route is still a pleasure. Have your breakfast at the picnic site before you proceed. The next half is even better for game viewing. Drive slowly and stop at the bird hide.

Look out for predators along the Ngotso drainage line on the H1-4. The last section before Satara is another hotspot. Watch for cheetah that dwell on these open plains. Lion and hyena are also often seen here. After Satara, the H7 is usually teeming with predators, grazers and browsers.

N'wanetsi Picnic Site (153 km; ± 6 hours)   ★★★★★

H7; H1-3 south; S100; S41 south; N'wanetsi; H6; H1-3 to Satara; back on the H7

Bobbejaan Krans (43 km; ± 2 hours)   ★★★★

H7; S106; lookout; back on the H7

The **Bobbejaan Krans** circuit is ideal for a short and slow afternoon drive. Notice the Rabelais Hut which is a historical site on the S106. The stark difference in vegetation on the three 'legs' of the route attracts different kinds of game. Observe how bird species also differ according to the habitat.

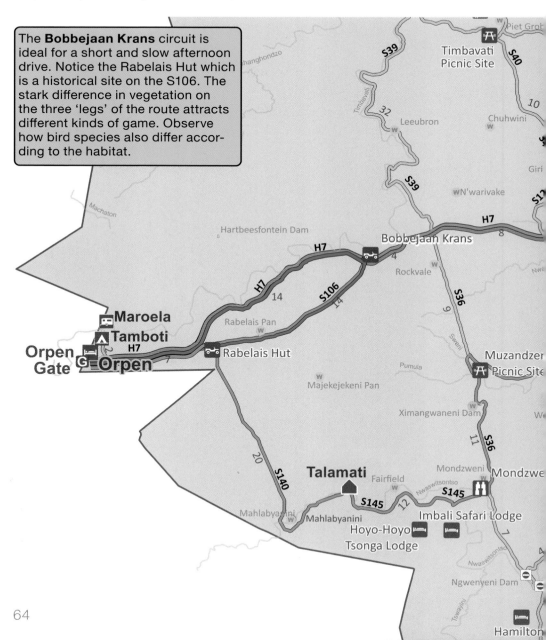

Muzandzeni Picnic Site (130 km; ± 5.5 hours) ★★★

H7; S140; S145; S36 north; Muzandzeni; S36; S126; H1-3; H7

The route to **N'wanetsi** via the S100 is pleasant and relaxing. Expect predators anywhere along the way. For successful game viewing, slow down and look deep into the bush. The route traverses several ecozones. Zebra and blue wildebeest are known to migrate northwards to this area before winter for better grazing and fresher water. With the onset of the summer rains, they slowly return to their summer grazing plains in the vicinity of the Mlondozi Dam in the south. Hotspots along the way are the riverine bush along the Timbavati, the lookout at Bobbejaan Krans, the Nsemani Dam, the marula woodland close to Satara, the entire S100, the N'wanetsi Picnic Site and the savanna woodland for giraffe and elephant on the H6. Consider a quick detour to Sweni Hide while you are at N'wanetsi.

The **Muzandzeni** circuit follows the zebra and wildebeest herds on the Talamati Plains. The Mahlabyanini Waterhole on the N'waswitsontso drainage line is a hotspot and so is the Fairfield Waterhole. Spend some time watching game at the dams on the S36. Expect to see zebra, wildebeest, buffalo and elephant herds, lion, hyena (if you are early), cheetah and perhaps wild dog. Look out for giraffe that feed on acacia trees. Muzandzeni Picnic Site is a pleasant place to have a picnic breakfast and stretch your legs. Thorn thickets along the first section of the S126 make game viewing difficult but further on – as the road follows the Sweni River – the vegetation opens up and viewing becomes extremely good with the likelihood of giraffe, leopard and lion sightings. Notice the thick stand of northern lala palms on the floodplain near the H1-3. Look out for rare sable and tsessebe.

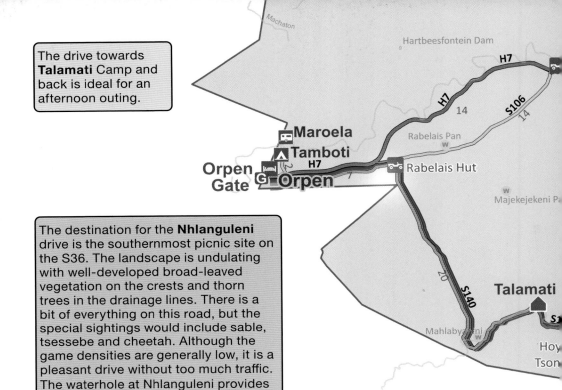

The drive towards **Talamati** Camp and back is ideal for an afternoon outing.

The destination for the **Nhlanguleni** drive is the southernmost picnic site on the S36. The landscape is undulating with well-developed broad-leaved vegetation on the crests and thorn trees in the drainage lines. There is a bit of everything on this road, but the special sightings would include sable, tsessebe and cheetah. Although the game densities are generally low, it is a pleasant drive without too much traffic. The waterhole at Nhlanguleni provides a reliable source of water and therefore zebra and wildebeest are frequently spotted from the picnic site. Lion and cheetah also visit and kills are sometimes witnessed.

Talamati Plains (57 km; ± 2 hours) ★★★

H7; S106; S140 up to N'waswitsontso and back

Nhlanguleni Picnic Site (132 km; ± 5.5 hours) ★★★

H7; S106; S140; S145; S36 south; Nhlanguleni Picnic Site; back on the S36; H7

Tshokwane Picnic Site (190 km; ± 8 hours) ★★★★

H7; S106; S140; S145; S36 south; S125; H1-3 south; S35; S32; H10 west; H1-2 north; Tshokwane; S34; S36; S145; S140; S106 west; H7

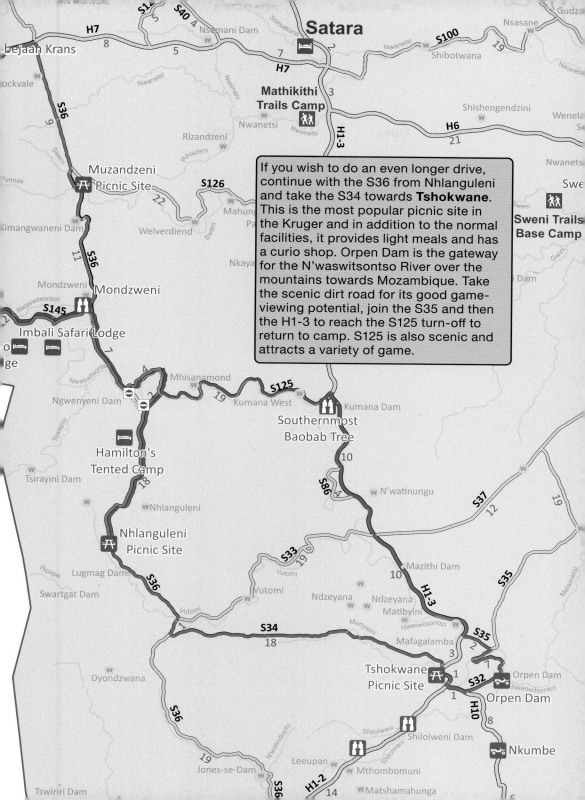

If you wish to do an even longer drive, continue with the S36 from Nhlanguleni and take the S34 towards **Tshokwane**. This is the most popular picnic site in the Kruger and in addition to the normal facilities, it provides light meals and has a curio shop. Orpen Dam is the gateway for the N'waswitsontso River over the mountains towards Mozambique. Take the scenic dirt road for its good game-viewing potential, join the S35 and then the H1-3 to reach the S125 turn-off to return to camp. S125 is also scenic and attracts a variety of game.

SKUKUZA ROUTES

- Skukuza is situated in the heart of Big Five territory and you can expect to see any of these on the roads close by.
- The camp is surrounded by mixed woodland and thorn thickets that occur mostly in the lower contours of the Sabie River catchment areas.
- Predators and scavengers such as lion, leopard, wild dog, cheetah and hyena can be encountered near the camp.
- The Stevenson-Hamilton Memorial Museum houses many interesting artefacts; famous among them is the knife with which ranger Harry Wolhuter single-handedly killed a lion and so saved his own life.

CLOSEST GET-OUT PLACES
- **Lake Panic on the S42** – no ablutions, no picnic facilities.
- **Nkuhlu Picnic Site on the H4-1** – ablutions, small shop, gas braais for hire, take a picnic basket or buy basic food items or meals.
- **Tshokwane Picnic Site on the H1-2** – ablutions, small shop, gas braais for hire, take a picnic basket or buy basic food items or meals.
- **Orpen** Memorial Koppie – no ablutions, no picnic facilities.
- **Kruger Tablets** – no ablutions, no picnic facilities.

PRIME DRINKING PLACES CLOSEST TO THE CAMP
- **Lake Panic** on the S42 (off the H11): 5.5 km.
- **Sabie River frontage** along the H4-1 and the S3.
- **Low-water bridge over the Sabie River** on the H1-2.
- **De Laporte Waterhole** on the H1-1 (5 km from the camp).
- **Renosterkoppies Waterhole** on the S114 (12 km from the camp).
- **Transport Dam** on the H1-1 (22 km from the camp).
- **N'waswitshaka Waterhole** on the S65 (24 km from the camp).

PRIME ROADS
- H1-1; H1-2; H3; H11; H4-2; S1; S3; S114; S83; S76; S65.

Lake Panic (11 km; ± 0.5 hours) ★★★★

H11; S42; Lake Panic and back

Waterhole Loop (44 km; ± 2 hours) ★★★★

H11; S1; S65; causeway over N'waswitshaka Waterhole; H1-1 east

Sabie Loop (34 km; ± 1.5 hours) ★★★★

H1-2; H12; high-water bridge; H4-1 west

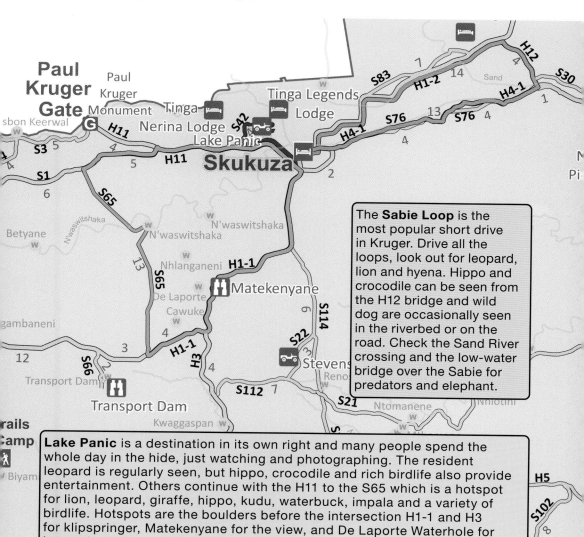

The **Sabie Loop** is the most popular short drive in Kruger. Drive all the loops, look out for leopard, lion and hyena. Hippo and crocodile can be seen from the H12 bridge and wild dog are occasionally seen in the riverbed or on the road. Check the Sand River crossing and the low-water bridge over the Sabie for predators and elephant.

Lake Panic is a destination in its own right and many people spend the whole day in the hide, just watching and photographing. The resident leopard is regularly seen, but hippo, crocodile and rich birdlife also provide entertainment. Others continue with the H11 to the S65 which is a hotspot for lion, leopard, giraffe, hippo, kudu, waterbuck, impala and a variety of birdlife. Hotspots are the boulders before the intersection H1-1 and H3 for klipspringer, Matekenyane for the view, and De Laporte Waterhole for leopard and lion.

Pretoriuskop Camp (158 km; ± 6 hours) ★★★★

H1-1; Transport Dam; Pretoriuskop; H1-1; S7; S3; S1 east; H11

Afsaal Trader's Rest (97 km; ± 4 hours) ★★★★

H1-1; H3; Afsaal; H3 north; S113; S23 south; Biyamiti Weir; turn back to the S114 north; H1-1

Hotspots on the route to **Pretoriuskop** are the De Laporte Waterhole for leopard, lion and hyena; the Matekenyane Hill for the scenery; the klipkoppies for klipspringer; the Transport Dam for hyena, cheetah, lion, buffalo, elephant, waterbuck, kudu, impala and good birding; the Napi Koppies for klipspringer and a historical sighting; the Shitlhave Dam for sable and other antelope.
The S10 provides sightings of baboon and leopard; the Nyamvundwa Dam has fish eagle, hippo and cheetah; the rest of the S1 has hyena and lion, and you might see leopard on the H11.

Paul Kruger Gate

Phabeni Gate

N'watinwambu · Mashukele
Doispan
Nyamundwa
Phabeni
Nyamundwa Dam
Albasini Ruins
Lisbon Keerwal
Betyane

Mlegeni
Mtshawu Dam
Shigambaneni

Mester Dam
Wolhuter
Transport Dam
Napi Dam

Numbi Gate
Foley Dam
Shitlhave Dam

Napi Trails Base Camp

Kwa Mcosheni
Manungu
Biyamiti

Willem

Pretoriuskop

Afsaal Trader's Post is both a historical and picnic site. A curio shop offers coffee and light meals. The Biyamiti Weir on the S114 is a hotspot on this route, but avoid the shortcut H2-2 to reach the S114.
Hotspots: De Laporte Waterhole for predators; Matekenyane for the views; Kwaggaspan for predators and general game; the area around Jock Safari Lodge and Afsaal for predators; S113 for cheetah; S23 for cheetah, lion, klipspringer and buffalo; the Renosterkoppies for leopard and lion, elephant and kudu.

Newu Dam
Renos

Nkuhlu Picnic Site (86 km; ± 3 hours) ★ ★ ★ ★ ★

H4-1; south on to S21; S114; S22; S122; H3; H1-1 north

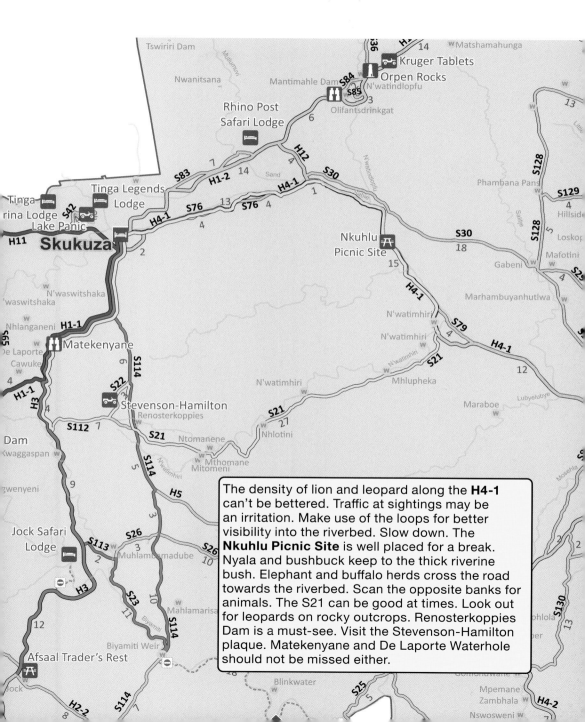

The density of lion and leopard along the **H4-1** can't be bettered. Traffic at sightings may be an irritation. Make use of the loops for better visibility into the riverbed. Slow down. The **Nkuhlu Picnic Site** is well placed for a break. Nyala and bushbuck keep to the thick riverine bush. Elephant and buffalo herds cross the road towards the riverbed. Scan the opposite banks for animals. The S21 can be good at times. Look out for leopards on rocky outcrops. Renosterkoppies Dam is a must-see. Visit the Stevenson-Hamilton plaque. Matekenyane and De Laporte Waterhole should not be missed either.

Tshokwane via Nhlanguleni (140 km; ± 6 hours) ★★★★

H1-2; S84; S36 to Nhlanguleni Picnic Site; back on S36; S33 east; H1-3 south; Tshokwane; H1-2

Tshokwane Picnic Site (88 km; ± 3.5 hours) ★★★★

H1-2; Mantimahle; Olifantsdrinkgat; Leeupan; Tshokwane and back on the H1-2

Golden Triangle (135 km; ± 5.5 hours) ★★★★★

H1-2; Tshokwane; H10; Lower Sabie; H4-1 to Skukuza

Lower Sabie Camp (100 km; ± 4 hours) ★★★★★

H4-1; Nkuhlu Picnic Site; H4-1; Sunset Dam; Lower Sabie; back via H4-1

The area **north of Skukuza** is characterised by thorn thickets on the lower contours, while mixed knob-thorn and marula form the dominant vegetation elsewhere. This is favoured habitat for larger birds of prey. Elephants and giraffes are regularly seen browsing while baboons and monkeys keep to the mature riverine vegetation. The hotspots on the H1-2 include the low-water bridges over the Sabie and Sand Rivers and riverbeds; the area around the Mantimahle Dam in the wet season; the Olifantsdrinkgat; the Orpen Rocks and the Kruger Memorial Tablets; as well as Leeupan in the wet season. Look out for lion, cheetah and sable. Don't miss Jones-se-Dam on the S36. The Lugmag Dam on the Ripape River is broken and contains no water. In the wet season this is a marshy area with waterbuck in abundance. **Nhlanguleni Picnic Site** overlooks a drinking spot where zebra, wildebeest and impala can be seen drinking in the distance, while lion and cheetah may also be around.

The S33 takes you to **Tshokwane** for a light meal served by the small shop or a picnic under huge shade trees.

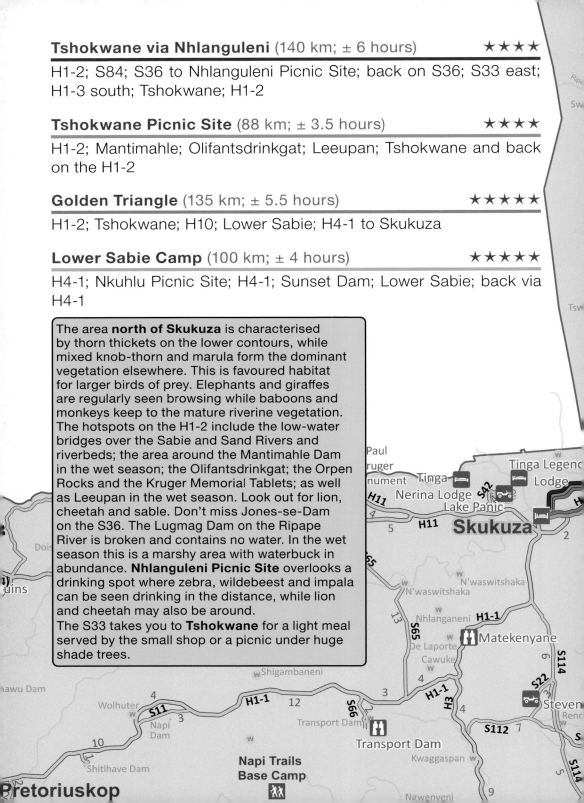

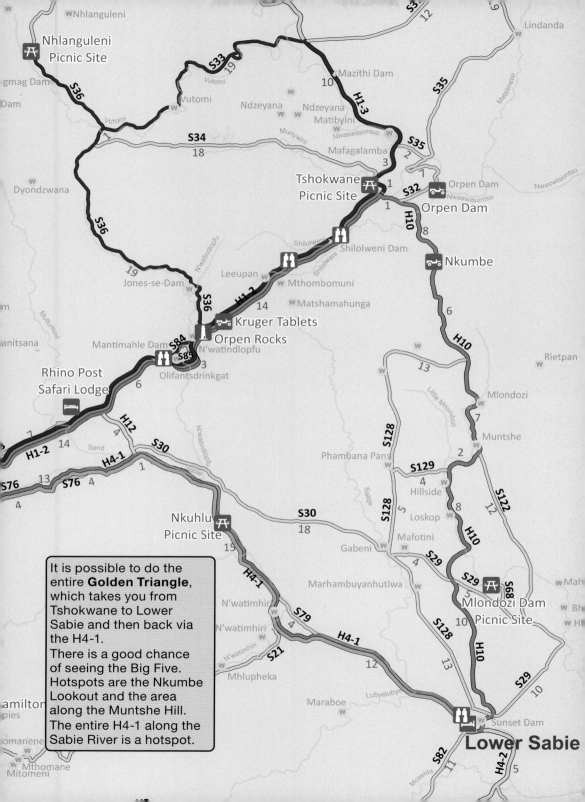

It is possible to do the entire **Golden Triangle**, which takes you from Tshokwane to Lower Sabie and then back via the H4-1.
There is a good chance of seeing the Big Five. Hotspots are the Nkumbe Lookout and the area along the Muntshe Hill.
The entire H4-1 along the Sabie River is a hotspot.

LOWER SABIE ROUTES

- The camp is surrounded by mixed woodland with sweet grazing; knob-thorn and marula woodlands are dense in places with pockets of grassland; a good game-viewing habitat.
- The leaves of these trees have a high concentration of tannin, which makes them unpalatable for most wildlife species, but kudu and black rhino seem to have a liking for them. Porcupines feed on their bark and are often seen on guided night drives in this area.
- Cheetah favour the grassland areas.
- The underlying geology is basalt and yields loam soils.
- Large numbers of animals are attracted to the abundance of water and sweet grass.
- This is Big Five country at its best.
- Excellent birding in the camp and at Sunset Dam.
- The grasslands around the Muntshe Hill are home to some of the largest zebra and wildebeest herds.

CLOSEST GET-OUT PLACES

- **Mlondozi Dam** – ablutions, cold drinks for sale, gas braais for hire, take a picnic basket.
- **Ntandanyathi Hide** – no ablutions, no picnic facilities.
- **Nkuhlu Picnic Site** – ablutions, small shop, gas braais for hire, take a picnic basket or buy basic food items or meals.

PRIME DRINKING PLACES CLOSEST TO THE CAMP

- **Sunset Dam** (1 km from camp); Sabie River frontage north and south of the camp; bridge over the Sabie River south of the camp.
- **Mlondozi Dam** (18 km)
- **Ntandanyathi Hide** (12 km)
- **Duke Waterhole** (15 km)

PRIME ROADS

- H4-1 north, tarred; H4-2 south, tarred; H10 to Tshokwane, tarred; S28 south, dirt.

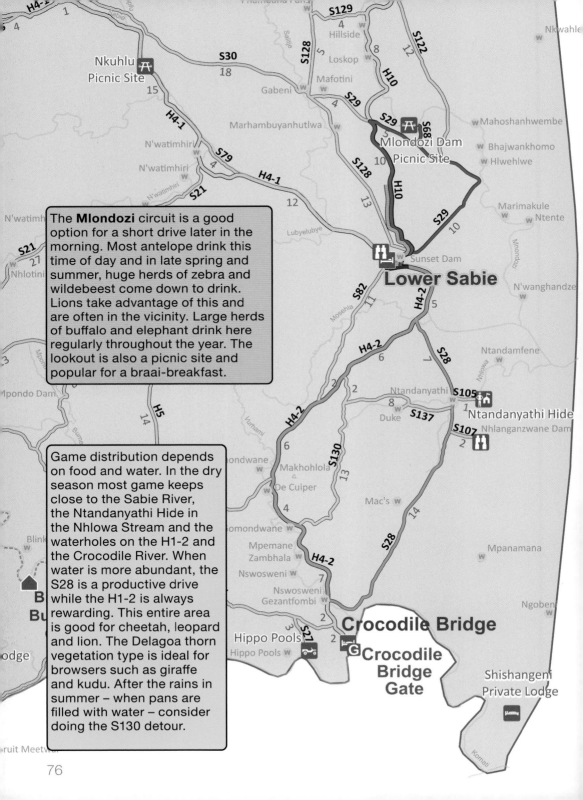

The **Mlondozi** circuit is a good option for a short drive later in the morning. Most antelope drink this time of day and in late spring and summer, huge herds of zebra and wildebeest come down to drink. Lions take advantage of this and are often in the vicinity. Large herds of buffalo and elephant drink here regularly throughout the year. The lookout is also a picnic site and popular for a braai-breakfast.

Game distribution depends on food and water. In the dry season most game keeps close to the Sabie River, the Ntandanyathi Hide in the Nhlowa Stream and the waterholes on the H1-2 and the Crocodile River. When water is more abundant, the S28 is a productive drive while the H1-2 is always rewarding. This entire area is good for cheetah, leopard and lion. The Delagoa thorn vegetation type is ideal for browsers such as giraffe and kudu. After the rains in summer – when pans are filled with water – consider doing the S130 detour.

Sunset Dam (2 km; 5 min) ★★★★★
H4-1

Bridge Below the Camp (5 km; 10 min) ★★★★
H10

Mlondozi Dam (28 km; ± 1.5 hours) ★★★★
H4-2; H10; S29; S68 to picnic site; S29 east; back via H10

Crocodile Bridge Camp (80 km; ± 3 hours) ★★★★
H4-2; Gomondwane; Crocodile Bridge; back via S28; H4-2

Short Golden Triangle (110 km; ± 4.5 hours) ★★★★

H10; H1-2 north; Tshokwane; back via H1-2; H12; H4-1 south back to camp

Long Golden Triangle (135 km; ± 6 hours) ★★★★

H10; H1-2 north; Tshokwane; H1-2 south to Skukuza and back to camp via H4-1

Skukuza Camp (143 km; ± 6 hours) ★★★★★

H4-1; Nkuhlu Picnic Site; Skukuza; back via H1-2; H12; turn off onto S30; continue straight over to S29; S68 to Mlondozi Dam; S29; H10

Skukuza via Renosterkoppies (113 km; ± 5 hours) ★★★★

H4-1; S21; S114 north; Renosterkoppies Waterhole; S22; S112 west; north onto H3; H1-1; Skukuza; back to Lower Sabie via H4-1

Game viewing and birding are usually good along the Sabie River because of the year-round availability of water. The highest density of leopard in the park occurs along the Sabie River. Regular lion sightings can be expected. Hyena have dens along this stretch. They are mainly seen early in the morning.

If you want to get away from the crowds, the road to **Skukuza via the Renosterkoppies** is for you. The gravel road S21 is often corrugated. It is scenic and traverses rolling hills with occasional granite outcrops, mixed knob-thorn and marula woodland with pockets of mixed grazing and thorn thickets along the lower contours. Visit the Stevenson-Hamilton Historic Site, which has a wonderful view over the southern bushveld. Baboons are often seen on the huge boulders. Elephant, buffalo, lion, leopard and a variety of antelope visit the dam.

Paul Kruger Gate
Paul Kruger Monument
Lisbon Keerwal
Tinga
Tinga Legend
Nerina Lodge
Lodge
Lake Panic
Skukuza
H11
Betyane
N'waswitshaka
N'waswitshaka
Nhlanganeni
H1-1
Matekenyane
De Laporte
Cawuke
Stevens
Renos
Transport Dam
Kwaggaspan
S112
Ngwenyeni
Jock Safari Lodge

The **long and short Golden Triangle Routes** are among the most popular in the park. The roads traverse several ecozones. Both routes have Tshokwane as a destination. Drive slowly so you don't miss special sightings. The H10 is a scenic drive across the eastern grasslands and into the Lebombo Mountain range. Look out for common reedbuck along the drainage line between the S129 and S29 intersections – one of only a few places to spot this antelope.

The route that includes the **S30** is another favourite. Drive along all the loops to check for game in the riverbed. This side of the Sabie River has a different ambience to the other side. The huge trees are impressive. This less-travelled road is a gem that simply must be explored.

Nhlanguleni Picnic Site

Tshokwane Picnic Site

Orpen Dam

Nkumbe

Shilolweni Dam

Leeupan

Mthombomuni

Matshamahunga

Kruger Tablets

Orpen Rocks

N'watindlopfu

Olifantsdrinkgat

Mantimahle Dam

Jones-se-Dam

Rhino Post Safari Lodge

Rietpan

Mlondozi

Muntshe

Phambana Pans

Hillside

Loskop

Mafotini

Gabeni

Nkuhlu Picnic Site

Marhambuyanhutlwa

Mlondozi Dam Picnic Site

Mahoshanhv

Bhajwankh

Hlwehlwe

N'watimhiri

N'watimhiri

N'watimhiri

Mhlupheka

Maraboe

Lubyelubye

Sunset Dam

Lower Sabie

Marimak

N'watimhiri

Nhlotini

Hamilton

Mthomane Mitomeni

Mpondo Dam

Mpondo Mpies

Ntandanyathi

Ntandamfen

Dyondzwana

gmag Dam

Dam

Nwaswitsontso

Nwaswitsontso

Nwaswitsontso

Little Mlondozi

Saljle

Sand

S33

S36

S36

S84

S85

S32

H10

H10

H10

H10

H10

H10

H1-2

H1-2

H1-2

H12

H4-1

H4-1

H4-1

H4-1

H4-2

S30

S30

S30

S76

S76

S76

S79

S21

S21

S128

S128

S128

S128

S129

S122

S29

S29

S29

S68

S26

S102

S28

S105

1

1

1

8

6

19

14

3

4

1

6

7

14

13

4

1

18

13

4

2

7

13

4

8

12

4

8

10

13

10

12

5

27

13

8

7

6

8

CROCODILE BRIDGE ROUTES

- Game densities near the camp are probably the highest in the park.
- The camp is surrounded by a typical flat landscape with soils originating from basalt. The grasses are therefore sweet and palatable and huge marula and knob-thorn trees dot the plains.
- Routes from this camp offer some of the best chances of encountering the Big Five on a single drive.

CLOSEST GET-OUT PLACES

- **Hippo Pools** – no ablution facilities, leave vehicle and approach river with the resident guide.
- **Ntandanyathi Bird Hide** – no ablution facilities.

PRIME DRINKING PLACES CLOSEST TO THE CAMP

- The **Crocodile River**, especially the S27 to the Hippo Pools (8 km); **Gezantfombi Pool** in the Vurhami Stream on the first section of the H4-2; **Gomondwane Waterhole** on the H4-2 and H5 crossing the stream; several pans in the rainy season on the S130; **Duke Waterhole** on the S137; **Ntandanyathi Hide** entrance road from the S28; **Mpondo Dam** on the S102.

PRIME ROADS

- H4-2 – tarred, a lot of traffic; S28 – dirt road, excellent visibility.

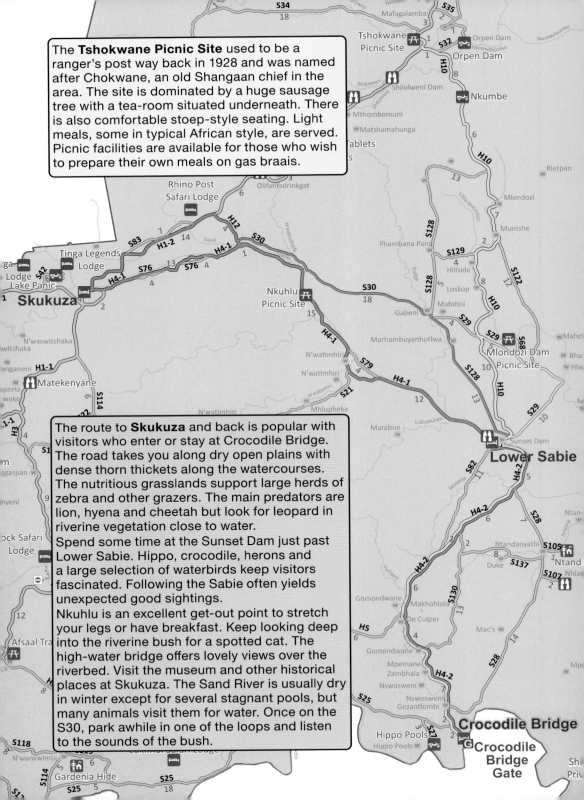

The **Tshokwane Picnic Site** used to be a ranger's post way back in 1928 and was named after Chokwane, an old Shangaan chief in the area. The site is dominated by a huge sausage tree with a tea-room situated underneath. There is also comfortable stoep-style seating. Light meals, some in typical African style, are served. Picnic facilities are available for those who wish to prepare their own meals on gas braais.

The route to **Skukuza** and back is popular with visitors who enter or stay at Crocodile Bridge. The road takes you along dry open plains with dense thorn thickets along the watercourses. The nutritious grasslands support large herds of zebra and other grazers. The main predators are lion, hyena and cheetah but look for leopard in riverine vegetation close to water.

Spend some time at the Sunset Dam just past Lower Sabie. Hippo, crocodile, herons and a large selection of waterbirds keep visitors fascinated. Following the Sabie often yields unexpected good sightings.

Nkuhlu is an excellent get-out point to stretch your legs or have breakfast. Keep looking deep into the riverine bush for a spotted cat. The high-water bridge offers lovely views over the riverbed. Visit the museum and other historical places at Skukuza. The Sand River is usually dry in winter except for several stagnant pools, but many animals visit them for water. Once on the S30, park awhile in one of the loops and listen to the sounds of the bush.

Tshokwane Picnic Site (196 km; ± 8 hours) ★★★★

H4-2; Lower Sabie; H10; Orpen Dam; S32; H1-2; Tshokwane; back via H10; S29; S68 to Mlondozi; S29 east; H4-2

Skukuza Camp (181 km; ± 7 hours) ★★★★★

H4-2, H4-1; Nkuhlu; Skukuza; H1-2; H12; S30; S128; H10 south; Lower Sabie; back via H4-2

The first part of the road along the S25 is rich in game. Drive slowly to avoid missing any predators that may be around. As you get to the S26 junction, notice how the vegetation has changed. This is because of the crossing at the Bume River. The Bume Road to Mpondo Dam passes through monotonous broad-leaved country before the S102 branches off. The **Mpondo Dam** offers a permanent water source for the game in that vicinity. Predators track their prey and can therefore be expected. The H5 follows part of the old railroad to Skukuza. Game along this road is sparse.

The gravel road to **Berg-en-Dal** can be rewarding but is often in bad condition. It passes through several vegetation zones and good game viewing is inconsistent. Look out for the smaller creatures such as dwarf mongoose which are entertaining to watch. Birds of prey are often seen. Big herds of buffalo and elephant may cross the road on their way to drink at the Crocodile River. The S110, S114 and S121 are all usually interesting but the S120 should be avoided if you are driving a low-clearance vehicle.

Berg-en-Dal (134 km; ± 5 hours) ★★★★

S25; S27 to Hippo Pools; S25; S114; S110; Berg-en-Dal; S110; S120; S121; S25

Mpondo Dam (64 km; ± 2.5 hours) ★★★

S25; S26; S102 to Mpondo Dam; back via H5; H4-2

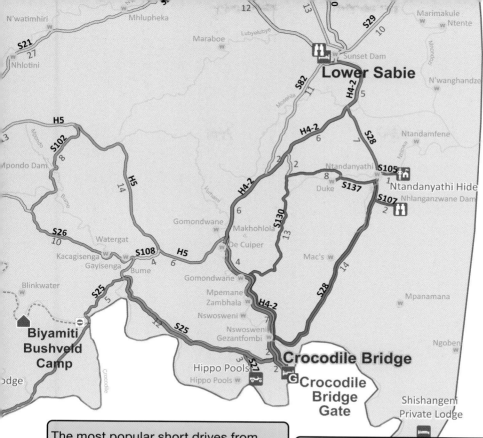

The most popular short drives from Crocodile Bridge follow the tarred road H4-2 and return with the gravel S28. The hotspots along the longer loop up to **Lower Sabie** include all the waterholes on the Vurhami River, especially Gezantfombi; the Sabie River front; the view from the bridge over the Sabie and the Sunset Dam. On the way back via the S28, visit the Ntandanyathi Hide. Along the S107 there is always game despite the dam being broken and holding no water.

The short circuit to the Duke Waterhole is particularly good in summer when the many-stemmed false-thorns on the Gomondwane Loop are in leaf and the pans are filled with water. Driving along this narrow track takes you into a wonder-world that differs from the rest of the savanna. Park at one of the pans and wait to see if there is any activity. The Duke Waterhole usually has no water but the drive is worthwhile.

Lower Sabie Camp (75 km; ± 3 hours)   ★★★★

H4-2; Lower Sabie; H4-2; back via S28; H4-2

Duke Waterhole (53 km; ± 2 hours)   ★★★★

H4-2; S28; S107 and back to S28; Ntandanyathi Hide; S28 south; S137; Duke Waterhole; S137; S130 south; H4-2

PRETORIUSKOP ROUTES

- The camp is situated within a landscape referred to as Pretorius-kop sourveld.
- The rainfall and the altitude here are the highest of all camps in the park. This results in tall grass and thick bush, making game spotting difficult.
- Large bare granite domes are typical, while silver cluster-leaf woodlands dominate the vegetation.
- The underlying geology is granite.
- In summer, grasses grow high and visibility is low.
- There are plenty of white rhino, buffalo, kudu and predators such as lion and leopard.
- Look out for sable, eland and tsessebe.

CLOSEST GET-OUT PLACES
- S1 (S04) at **Albasini Ruins** – no ablutions, no picnic facilities.
- H2-2 at **Afsaal** – ablutions, gas braais for hire, cold drinks for sale, take a picnic basket.

PRIME DRINKING PLACES CLOSEST TO THE CAMP
- **Shitlhave Dam** on H1-1 (8 km); **Mestel Dam** on S3 south (15 km).
- **Nyamundwa** on S1 (34 km); **Transport Dam** on H1-1 (34 km).

PRIME ROADS
- S14 – Fayi Loop; H1-1 to Skukuza; H2-2 to Afsaal; S7 – Shabeni Loop.

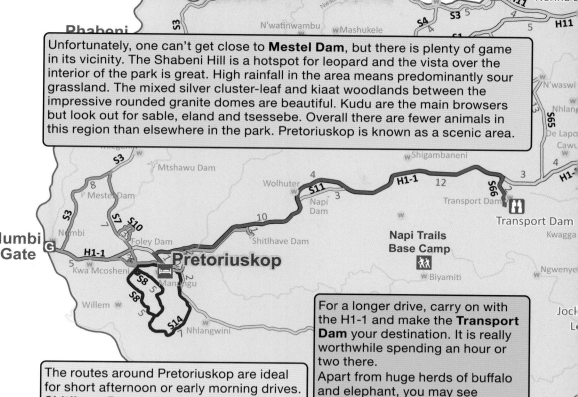

Unfortunately, one can't get close to **Mestel Dam**, but there is plenty of game in its vicinity. The Shabeni Hill is a hotspot for leopard and the vista over the interior of the park is great. High rainfall in the area means predominantly sour grassland. The mixed silver cluster-leaf and kiaat woodlands between the impressive rounded granite domes are beautiful. Kudu are the main browsers but look out for sable, eland and tsessebe. Overall there are fewer animals in this region than elsewhere in the park. Pretoriuskop is known as a scenic area.

The routes around Pretoriuskop are ideal for short afternoon or early morning drives. **Shitlhave Dam** is a popular destination. In the early morning there is a chance of seeing predators and buffalo. Later on, the antelope of the area come down to drink. This is where you may see the shy and elusive eland, sable and tsessebe.

For a longer drive, carry on with the H1-1 and make the **Transport Dam** your destination. It is really worthwhile spending an hour or two there.
Apart from huge herds of buffalo and elephant, you may see cheetah, lion, hyena, jackal and all the antelope of the area.
This is the ideal spot to watch animal behaviour and interaction. Birds will keep you entertained if larger game is absent.

Mestel Dam (28 km; ± 1 hour)   ★★★

H1-1 west; S7; S10; Shabeni; S7; S3 south; Mestel Dam; S3 south; H1-1 east to camp

Transport Dam (64 km; ± 2.5 hours)   ★★★★

H1-1 east; S66 to Transport Dam and back

Fayi Loop (26 km; ± 1 hour)   ★★★★

S14; S8

Shitlhave Dam (10 km; 0.5 hours)   ★★★

H1-1; Shitlhave Dam; H1-1 back to camp

Tshokwane Picnic Site (160 km; ± 6 hours) ★★★★

H1-1; Skukuza; H1-2; Tshokwane; S34; S36 south (via Jones-se-Dam); H1-2 south; H12; H4-1 west; Skukuza; H1-1 back

Nkuhlu Picnic Site (156 km; ± 6 hours) ★★★★

H1-1; S7; S3; S1; H11; Skukuza; H4-1; Nkuhlu; H4-1; S21; S114 north; Renosterkoppies; S22; S112; H3 north; H1-1 west

Skukuza Camp (105 km; ± 4 hours) ★★★★

H1-1; Skukuza; H11; S1; S3 south; S7; H1-1 to camp

Afsaal via Skukuza (127 km; ± 5 hours) ★★★

H1-1; Skukuza; H1-1 south; S114; S112; H3 south up to Afsaal; west on H2-2

The circuit along the Voortrekker Road is of historical interest. Find Ship Mountain, Jock of the Bushveld and other historical plaques. This is one of only two H-roads which are not tarred. Breakfast at **Afsaal** can be memorable. The H3 is usually productive, especially in the vicinity of Jock Safari Lodge and the S113 (the Biyamiti drainage line). Reach **Skukuza** via the Renosterkoppies. Visit the historical sites at Skukuza Camp. On the H1-1, spend some time at the De Laporte Waterhole and the Transport Dam. Look for klipspringer on the granite koppies. Make a last detour to Shitlhave Dam before driving back to camp.

The **S7, S3, S1 loop** is another highly recommended route.

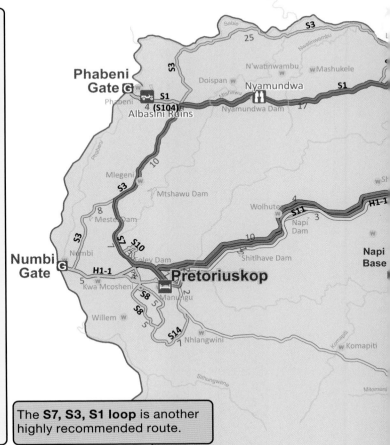

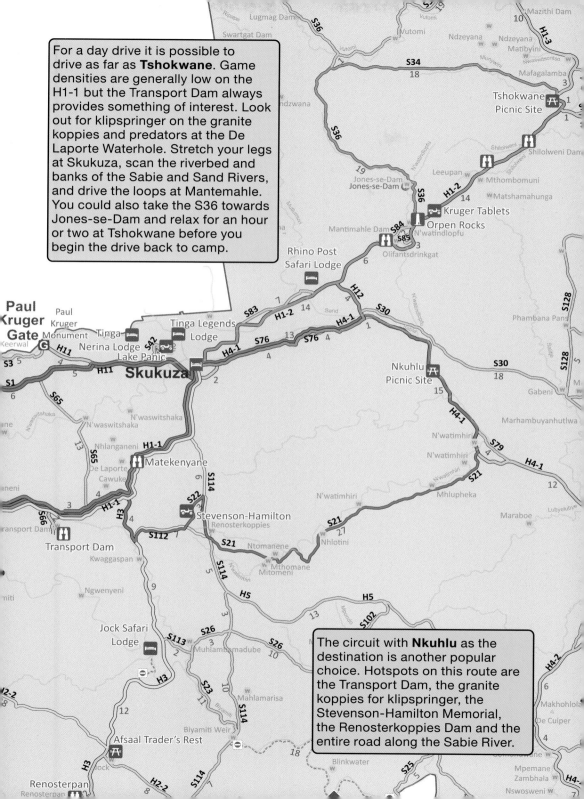

For a day drive it is possible to drive as far as **Tshokwane**. Game densities are generally low on the H1-1 but the Transport Dam always provides something of interest. Look out for klipspringer on the granite koppies and predators at the De Laporte Waterhole. Stretch your legs at Skukuza, scan the riverbed and banks of the Sabie and Sand Rivers, and drive the loops at Mantemahle. You could also take the S36 towards Jones-se-Dam and relax for an hour or two at Tshokwane before you begin the drive back to camp.

The circuit with **Nkuhlu** as the destination is another popular choice. Hotspots on this route are the Transport Dam, the granite koppies for klipspringer, the Stevenson-Hamilton Memorial, the Renosterkoppies Dam and the entire road along the Sabie River.

BERG-EN-DAL ROUTES

- In the vicinity of Berg-en-Dal, game densities are relatively low compared to other areas in the park but this does not always affect the variety of game species.
- Grasses on the crests and slopes are not as palatable as in the valleys, where most grazers will congregate.
- Broad-leaved vegetation (e.g. bushwillows) will attract browsers – expect to see kudu, elephant, impala and smaller antelope.
- Giraffe favour knob-thorn and these occur only in the valleys.
- Study the area map and find the places where there should be surface water.
- Leopard and hyaena are the prime predators close to the camp. Wild dog is sporadically seen, and lion less often in close proximity to the camp, but further northwards and eastwards.

CLOSEST GET-OUT PLACES

- **Afsaal Trader's Rest** – ablutions, gas braais for hire, cold drinks for sale, take a picnic basket, small shop, basic food items or meals.
- **Gardenia Hide** – no ablutions, no picnic facilities.

PRIME DRINKING PLACES CLOSEST TO THE CAMP

- Dam in front of reception; **Matjulu Waterhole**; H3 crossing over **Matjulu Stream**; bridge over **Crocodile River** at the **Malelane Gate**; bridge over the seasonal **Mhlambane River**; pools in the seasonal Mhlambane River along the S118 and S119; pan at the **Gardenia Hide**; **Renosterpan**; **Biyamiti Weir**; seasonal **Biyamiti River** with pools (crossing on H3 and S23 up to the weir). Animals cross the S114 and S25 on their way to the perennial Crocodile River.

PRIME ROADS

- S110 – the tarred part; H3 – the entire road; S118 and S119 – dirt; S114 – some stretches may be corrugated and unproductive; S25 – dirt road, carries much traffic, sometimes corrugated in places; S23 – dirt road; S120 – most scenic but rough surface.

Pretoriuskop (189 km; ± 7.5 hours)   ★★★

S110; H3; H2-2; Pretoriuskop; H1-1; Skukuza; H1-1; H3; S110

Skukuza Camp (144 km; ± 6 hours)   ★★★★

S110; H3; H1-1; Skukuza; either H1-2 or H4-1 to H12; H4-1 south;
Nkuhlu; H4-1 south; S21; S112; H3 south; S110

Crocodile Bridge (201 km; ± 8 hours)   ★★★

S110; S114; S25; Crocodile Bridge; H4-2; Lower Sabie; H4-1; S21;
S112; H3; S110

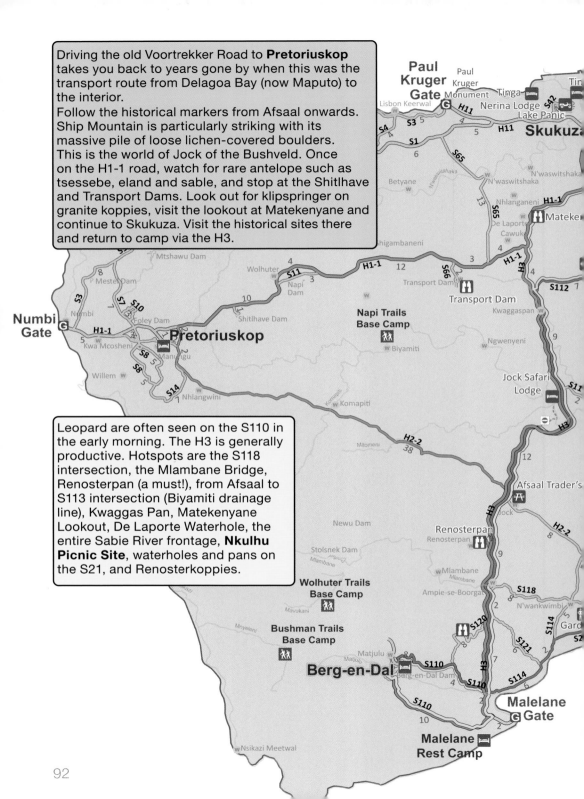

Driving the old Voortrekker Road to **Pretoriuskop** takes you back to years gone by when this was the transport route from Delagoa Bay (now Maputo) to the interior.

Follow the historical markers from Afsaal onwards. Ship Mountain is particularly striking with its massive pile of loose lichen-covered boulders. This is the world of Jock of the Bushveld. Once on the H1-1 road, watch for rare antelope such as tsessebe, eland and sable, and stop at the Shitlhave and Transport Dams. Look out for klipspringer on granite koppies, visit the lookout at Matekenyane and continue to Skukuza. Visit the historical sites there and return to camp via the H3.

Leopard are often seen on the S110 in the early morning. The H3 is generally productive. Hotspots are the S118 intersection, the Mlambane Bridge, Renosterpan (a must!), from Afsaal to S113 intersection (Biyamiti drainage line), Kwaggas Pan, Matekenyane Lookout, De Laporte Waterhole, the entire Sabie River frontage, **Nkulhu Picnic Site**, waterholes and pans on the S21, and Renosterkoppies.

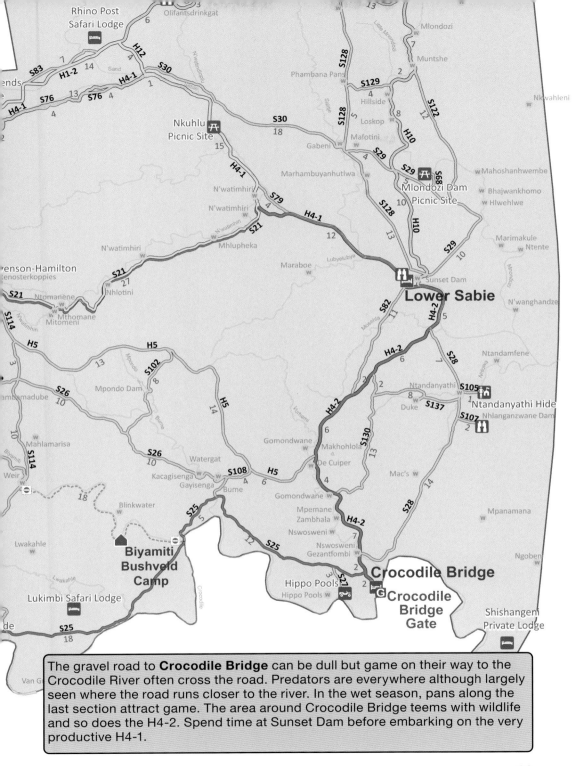

Rhino Post
Safari Lodge

Olifantsdrinkgat

Mlondozi

Little Mlondozi

Muntshe

S128

S83   H1-2   14   Sand   4   H12   S30

S129

Phambana Pans

H4-1

S76   13   S76   4   1

S128   Hillside

S122   Nkwahleni

S128   Loskop

H4-1

Nkuhlu
Picnic Site

S30
18   15

Mafotini

Gabeni

S29   4

Marhambuyanhutlwa

H10

S29   Mahoshanhwembe

H4-1

N'watimhiri

S79
4

N'watimhiri

S21

H4-1
12

Mlondozi Dam
Picnic Site

Bhajwankhomo

Hlwehlwe

S128   10

Marimakule

Ntente

N'watimhiri

Mhlupheka

Maraboe

Lubyekubye

S29   10

enson-Hamilton
enosterkoppies

S21
27

Nhlotini

Sunset Dam

Lower Sabie

N'wanghandze

S21   Ntomanene

Mthomane
Mitomeni

S82
11

H4-2
5

S114

H5   H5

S28

Ntandamfene

H5   13   S102

S26   10   Mpondo Dam

8

H5
14

H4-2
6

2

H4-2   6

S130
13

Ntandanyathi   S105

Duke   8   S137

Ntandanyathi Hide

S107   2   Nhlanganzwane Dam

ambamadube

S114

Mahlamarisa

S26   10

Watergat

H5   6

Kacagisenga
Gayisenga   S108   Bume

Weir

18

Blinkwater

S25   5

Biyamiti
Bushveld
Camp

Gomondwane

Makhohlola
De Cuiper

4

Gomondwane

Mac's

S28   14

Mpanamana

Mpemane
Zambhala

H4-2
7

Nswosweni

S25   12   S25

Nswosweni
Gezantfombi

2

Crocodile Bridge

Hippo Pools

S27

Crocodile
Bridge
Gate

Ngoben

Lwakahle

Lukimbi Safari Lodge

Lwakahle

Hippo Pools

Shishangeni
Private Lodge

S25
18

The gravel road to **Crocodile Bridge** can be dull but game on their way to the Crocodile River often cross the road. Predators are everywhere although largely seen where the road runs closer to the river. In the wet season, pans along the last section attract game. The area around Crocodile Bridge teems with wildlife and so does the H4-2. Spend time at Sunset Dam before embarking on the very productive H4-1.

93

Matjulu Waterhole (10 km; ± 30 min)   ★★★★
S110 dirt; Matjulu Waterhole; back on the S110

Afsaal Trader's Rest (144 km; ± 6 hours)   ★★★★
S110; S114; S25; S119; Gardenia Hide; S119; S118; H3 north; Afsaal; H3; S113; S23; S114 south; Biyamiti Weir; S114; S110

Gardenia Hide (10 km; ± 30 min)   ★★★★
S110; S114; S25; S119; Gardenia Hide; S119; S118; H3 south; S110

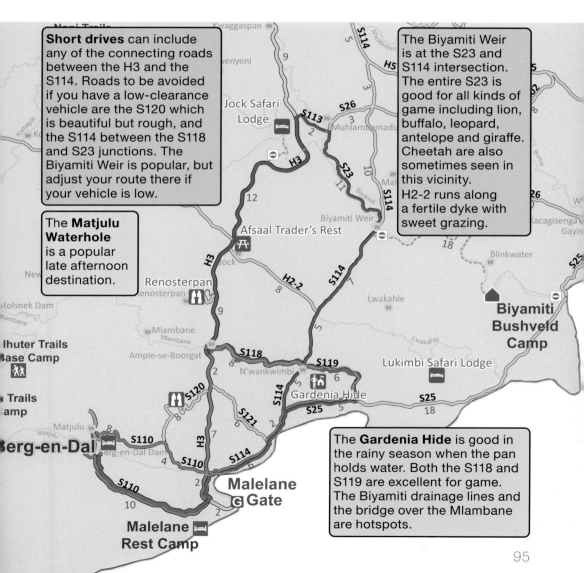

Short drives can include any of the connecting roads between the H3 and the S114. Roads to be avoided if you have a low-clearance vehicle are the S120 which is beautiful but rough, and the S114 between the S118 and S23 junctions. The Biyamiti Weir is popular, but adjust your route there if your vehicle is low.

The **Matjulu Waterhole** is a popular late afternoon destination.

The Biyamiti Weir is at the S23 and S114 intersection. The entire S23 is good for all kinds of game including lion, buffalo, leopard, antelope and giraffe. Cheetah are also sometimes seen in this vicinity. H2-2 runs along a fertile dyke with sweet grazing.

The **Gardenia Hide** is good in the rainy season when the pan holds water. Both the S118 and S119 are excellent for game. The Biyamiti drainage lines and the bridge over the Mlambane are hotspots.

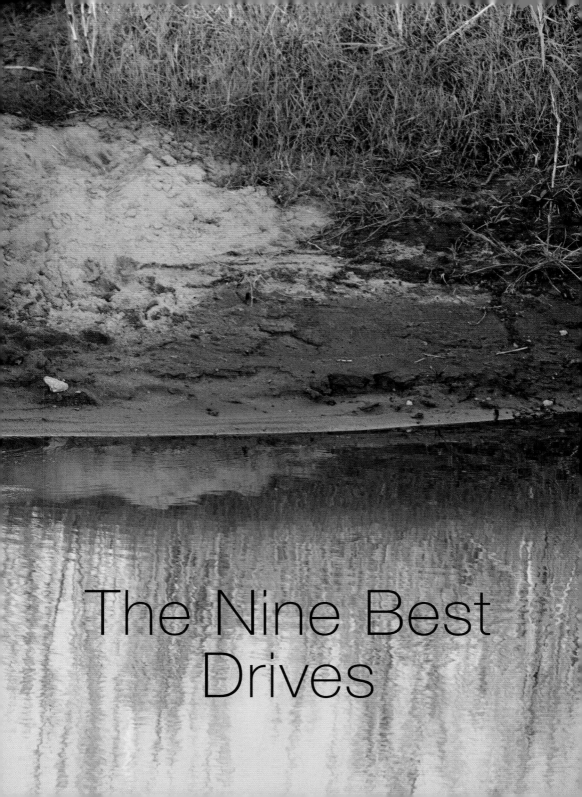

The Nine Best
Drives

THE NINE BEST DRIVES

There are many kinds of self-drive tourists in Kruger. Some are birders with birding stickers on their windows, others are tree-spotters ticking off species on a list, while others simply meander along enjoying the atmosphere. Then there are the photographers who act as if they have the right of way, and those who race between lion sightings like maniacs, hanging out of windows with selfie sticks, while others do their best to avoid lion sightings because they don't want to get stuck in traffic looking at people watching sleeping lions.

Likewise, you get a rich diversity of species in the park but they are not evenly distributed. There are roads that usually offer good sightings yet do not always meet expectations. This unpredictability is what makes game drives so exciting. You never know what you're going to get.

The best way to drive in Kruger is to slow down, relax and focus on the small things. When you're looking for the big things, remember the availability of surface water (dams, waterholes, rivers) greatly influences the movements and concentration of game, so check your map to see where these are and be more vigilant when you approach these areas. Tarred roads (H-roads), carry heavier traffic (and more inconsiderate drivers) than dirt roads (S-roads), which are generally more relaxing and offer an intimate bush experience.

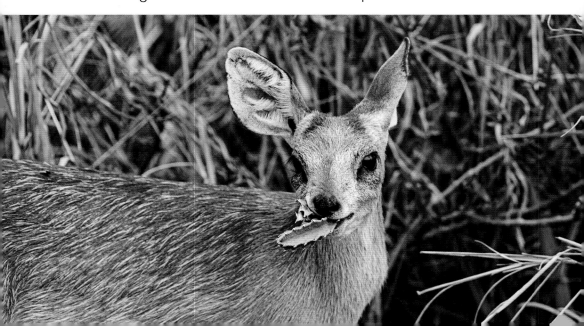

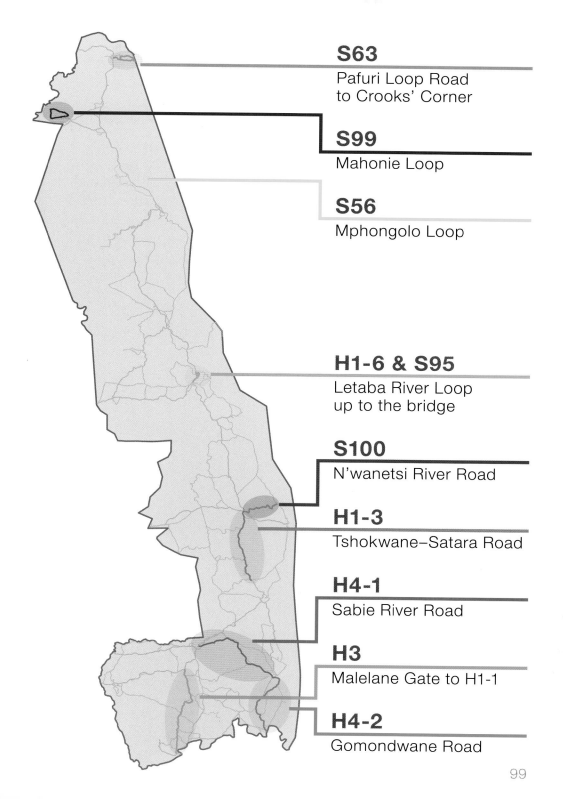

S63
Pafuri Loop Road
to Crooks' Corner

S99
Mahonie Loop

S56
Mphongolo Loop

H1-6 & S95
Letaba River Loop
up to the bridge

S100
N'wanetsi River Road

H1-3
Tshokwane–Satara Road

H4-1
Sabie River Road

H3
Malelane Gate to H1-1

H4-2
Gomondwane Road

NORTHERN KRUGER

S63 PAFURI LOOP ROAD TO CROOKS' CORNER

This is a birders' paradise. Yet the highlight of this loop is the confluence of the Luvuvhu and Limpopo Rivers where a small triangular tongue of land is wedged between three countries. Crooks' Corner is probably one of the most notorious historical places in the park. Ivory poachers, gun-runners, fugitives and others who were avoiding the law based themselves here so that they could simply hop over the border and place themselves out of legal reach. Today, birders and others visit the banks of the Luvuvhu to experience its tropical atmosphere, see the Sykes' monkey (the only place in the park where it can be found) and enjoy the variety of birds such as the crested guineafowl, Meve's starling and knob-tailed roller that only occur here. The all-time special sighting would be that of the Pel's fishing owl. The baobabs here are awe-inspiring but so are the fever trees, fig trees, ana trees, sausage trees and many others. The Pafuri Picnic Site has a special ambience, wonderful picnic facilities, excellent opportunities for birding and an informative open-air display centre.

S99 MAHONIE LOOP

The S99 is the botanical jewel of the north and was named after the many specimens of pod mahogany along this loop which circum-navigates the hill behind Punda Maria. The hill slopes also support an astounding diversity of plant species, several of which are unique to the park. The easiest trees to recognise are the large-fruited bushwillows with their big winged fruits; the baobabs so typical of Africa; the apple-leaf trees with gnarled trunks and pale green leaves; jackalberries with dense, roundish canopies; sycamore figs with huge, yellowish trunks and leadwood bushwillows which are tall and high-branching with pale grey bark that breaks up into small, regular snakeskin-like blocks. The Lebombo ironwood is found only here and along the Lebombo Mountains. The soil in this part of the park is sandy and well drained and in summer, it supports a wonderworld of flowering shrubs and annuals. Game sightings could include elephant, Sharpe's grysbok, impala, kudu, buffalo and a few others. Predators are around but are not often encountered. Bird diversity is great, so birding is rewarding.

S56 MPHONGOLO LOOP

North of Shingwedzi, the meandering S56 follows the Mphongolo River course where riverine forest is in stark contrast to the surrounding monotonous mopane plains. This is home to the rare Sharpe's grysbok which is often confused with steenbok, but which occupies a different kind of habitat. Numerous loops wander closer to the river bank and tsessebe – which are considered the fastest antelope in southern Africa and occur only on the northern mopane plains – are occasionally seen drinking at one of the pools. Buffalo and elephant herds, but also journeys of giraffe, may be seen in the riverbed. The route offers prime habitat for lion and leopard, although lower predator densities come with lower game concentrations. Birding is excellent for terrestrial, frugivorous and general bushveld species. Sightings of endangered raptors are always special. The Babalala Picnic Site is an all-time favourite and offers gas braais, tables and chairs, a kitchenette and clean ablutions.

CENTRAL KRUGER

H1-6 AND S95 LETABA RIVER LOOP
UP TO THE BRIDGE

The first few kilometres on the Letaba Camp side of the H1-6 and the S95 loop, running up to the bridge over the Letaba River are magical. The loop runs parallel to the Letaba River, offers splendid views over the wide river towards the opposite bank and is fringed by lush riverine bush. Here one can expect to see huge hippo pods and crocodiles sunning themselves on the bank, elephant, waterbuck, waterbirds, raptors and many others. Providing more action on the riverbank, monkeys and baboons entertain each other, while giraffe feed on the acacias and elephant bulls trudge along. The warthogs and impala go about their business, and bee-eaters swoop down to catch insects. The high bridge over the Letaba River shows the magnitude of this perennial waterway that can carry masses of water to the Olifants River after good rains. In times of drought, stagnant pools remain and are an important life-sustaining source of water along its entire course. Large quantities of sand are carried down with the water and deposited as sandbanks along the way.

S100 N'WANETSI RIVER ROAD

All the best conditions for game viewing are present on the N'wanetsi River Road: it runs parallel with the perennial river which has deep water-retaining pools; scenic riverine vegetation that is lush and beautiful; clay depressions and shallow pans that retain water in the rainy season; grassland savanna that is open, providing the best visibility; sweet grass, rich in minerals, attracting herds of impala, zebra, wildebeest, buffalo, waterbuck and elephant, as well as riverine vegetation which attracts giraffe, kudu, bushbuck and nyala. No wonder this is called supreme predator country because where prey is in such abundance, predators follow. In spite of the dusty gravel with its bumpy surface, this road is still one of the best places to see lion prides, leopard and hyena.

H1-3 TSHOKWANE TO SATARA ROAD

This is one of the best drives in central Kruger. Visibility is excellent and the road passes reliable water sources which means game is plentiful. The only problem with this road might be too much traffic. The landscape here is characterised by gently undulating plains without high ridges or hills. The reason for the abundance of game lies in the geology, soil and vegetation of the surrounding plains. Almost the entire road runs through fertile savanna plains which are underpinned by basalt, covered by a layer of calcrete. The grasses are therefore sweet and the landscape is mostly open with knob-thorn and marula as the dominant tree species. A few big dams and pans add to the attraction. In the region of the Kumana Dam, the southernmost naturally occurring baobab tree can be seen. This is prime country for giraffe but all other game occur in abundance.

SOUTHERN KRUGER

H4-1 SABIE RIVER ROAD

The main attractions of this road are the scenery, the abundance of game and the Sabie River it follows. *Sabisa* is the Swati word for 'frightening' and refers to the dangers of crossing this river with its slippery rocks and dangerous crocodiles. The views onto the riverbed are spectacular. Elephant, buffalo and grazers regularly cross the road on their way to water. Lion sightings often occur, and even the elusive leopard is regularly seen. The riverine forest attracts a plethora of birds, shy bushbuck, monkeys and baboons while the thicket vegetation into the interior is ideal habitat for black rhino. Hotspots are the high-water bridge over the Sabie, the Nkuhlu Picnic Site, Lubyelubye River crossing with the occasional appearance of sandstone favoured by lion and klipspringer, and the popular Sunset Dam where people spend hours watching birds, game and other people.

H3 MALELANE GATE TO H1-1

This drive initially takes you through a scenic mountainous area covered by broad-leaved vegetation, before it flattens out into gently undulating kudu country dotted with intermittent impala herds and the occasional predator. Look out for hyena that den under culverts, and wild dog that are seen from time to time. A hotspot is the bridge over the Mlambane River where visibility is good and elephant, lion, leopard and other game often linger. Don't ignore the turn-off to Renosterpan which takes you to a semi-permanent pan. A huge leadwood offers shade while watching game and birds from your vehicle. Afsaal Picnic Site has a shop, light meals, braai facilities and ablutions. The thornveld surrounding Afsaal is a particularly good game area with sweet grasses. Thereafter, the road enters the Biyamiti basin which is another hotspot. Scout for klipspringer on the koppies, as well as elephant, lion, zebra, kudu and impala in this area. Kwaggaspan, about nine kilometres further, is worth scanning carefully with binoculars.

H4-2 GOMONDWANE ROAD

The road into the park from the far southeast is part of the Southern Circle. It traverses the excellent grazing area surrounding the Crocodile Bridge Camp. Here the grass is sweet and palatable due to the underlying basalt soils. High concentrations of grazers attract predators of all kinds and many visitors encounter lion and leopard soon after entering the park. There is usually some animal activity at Gezantfombi and this road is also famous for good cheetah sightings. At times, wild dog den in the vicinity and then sightings are numerous and extremely rewarding. Closer to Lower Sabie, the road follows the Sabie River where leopard and other game are often seen. The road is steeped in history, being one of the first two-tracks into the park built by ranger CR de Laporte. Pioneering traders Joào Albasini (who was Portuguese) and Sardinelli (a Greek) had trading posts here long before it was a park and the Battle of Gomondwane was one of the first skirmishes between traders and Shangaan warriors.

THE ULTIMATE ROAD IN KRUGER

There are many more good roads in Kruger but the best one is the one you are driving on. Exceptional sightings can happen anywhere.

Notes
on Roads

H-ROADS

Road number	Name of road	Closest rest camp	Distance & rating
H1-1	Napi Road	Pretoriuskop, Skukuza	55 km ★★★★
H1-2	Skukuza–Tshokwane	Skukuza	39 km ★★★★
H1-3	Tshokwane–Satara	Satara	50 km ★★★★★
H1-4	Satara–Olifants River	Balule, Olifants Camp	39 km ★★★★
H1-5	Olifants River–Letaba	Olifants Camp, Letaba	28 km ★★★
H1-6 (1)	Letaba–Mopani	Letaba, Mopani, Shimuwini	43 km ★★★
H1-6 (2)	Mopani–Shingwedzi	Mopani, Bateleur, Shingwedzi	62 km ★★★
H1-7	Shingwedzi–H13-1	Shingwedzi, Sirheni	51 km ★★★
H1-8	H13-1–Luvuvhu River	Punda Maria	38 km ★★★
H1-9	Luvuvhu River–Pafuri Gate	Punda Maria	20 km ★★★
H2-2	Pretoriuskop	Pretoriuskop	44 km ★★★
H3	Malelane Gate–H1-1	Berg-en-Dal, Skukuza	49 km ★★★★
H4-1	Skukuza–Lower Sabie	Skukuza, Lower Sabie	43 km ★★★★★
H4-2	Gomondwane Road	Crocodile Bridge, Lower Sabie	35 km ★★★★
H5	Randspruit Road	Crocodile Bridge, Lower Sabie	33 km ★★★
H6	H1-3–N'wanetsi	Satara	19 km ★★★★
H7	Orpen Road	Orpen, Tamboti, Marula, Satara	45 km ★★★★★

Notes

Road number	Name of road	Closest rest camp	Distance & rating
H8	Olifants Camp Road	Balule, Olifants Camp	8 km ★★★
H9	Phalaborwa–Letaba Road	Letaba	51 km ★★★
H10	Lower Sabie–Tshokwane	Lower Sabie	39 km ★★★★★
H11	Kruger Gate–Skukuza	Skukuza	14 km ★★★
H12	Link between H4-1 and H1-2	Skukuza	5 km ★★★★
H13-1	Punda Maria Gate Road	Punda Maria	20 km ★★★
H13-2	Punda Maria Camp Road	Punda Maria	3 km ★★★
H14	Phalaborwa–Mopani Road	Mopani	53 km ★★★★
H15	Giriyondo	Letaba	25 km ★★★

S-ROADS

Road number	Name of road	Closest rest camp	Distance & rating
S1	Doispane Road	Pretoriuskop, Skukuza	43 km ★★★★
S3	Sabie River Road (West)	Skukuza	29 km ★★★★
S4	Link Road	Skukuza	4 km ★★★
S7	Link Road	Pretoriuskop	6 km ★★★
S8	Manungu Loop	Pretoriuskop	10 km ★★★
S10	Shabeni Loop	Pretoriuskop	3 km ★★★
S12	Girivana Loop	Satara, Orpen, Tamboti, Marula	5 km ★★★
S14	Fayi Loop	Pretoriuskop	7 km ★★★
S21	N'watimhiri Road	Skukuza, Lower Sabie	27 km ★★★★
S22	Stevenson-Hamilton	Skukuza	3 km ★★★★
S23	Biyamiti Loop	Berg-en-Dal, Skukuza	14 km ★★★★
S25	Crocodile River Road	Crocodile Bridge, Berg-en-Dal	43 km ★★★★
S26	Bume Road	Crocodile Bridge, Berg-en-Dal	20 km ★★★
S27	Hippo Pools Road	Crocodile Bridge	3 km ★★★★
S28	Nhlowa Road	Crocodile Bridge, Lower Sabie	24 km ★★★★
S29	Mhlondozi Road	Lower Sabie	18 km ★★★★
S30	Salitjie Road	Lower Sabie, Skukuza	18 km ★★★★

Notes

Road number	Name of road	Closest rest camp	Distance & rating
S32	Orpen Dam Road	Skukuza, Lower Sabie, Satara	2 km ★★★★
S33	Vutomi Road	Satara, Skukuza	17 km ★★★
S34	Munywini Road	Satara, Skukuza	19 km ★★★
S35	Lindanda Road	Satara, Skukuza	20 km ★★★
S36	Nhlanguleni–Muzandzeni Road	Skukuza, Satara, Talamati, Orpen, Marula, Tamboti	48 km ★★★★
S37	Trichardt Road	Satara	36 km ★★★★
S39	Timbavati Road	Satara, Olifants Camp, Balule, Tamboti, Marula, Orpen	60 km ★★★★
S40	Nsemani Road	Orpen, Tamboti, Marula, Satara	16 km ★★★
S41	Gudzani Road	Satara	29 km ★★★★★
S42	Lake Panic and Nursery	Skukuza	3 km ★★★★★
S44	Olifants Mountain Road	Olifants Camp	14 km ★★★
S46	Letaba River Road (South)	Letaba	21 km ★★★
S47	Mingerhout Dam Road	Letaba	29 km ★★★
S48	Tsendze Loop	Letaba, Mopani	17 km ★★★
S49	Parallel to H1-6	Mopani	8 km ★★★
S50	Nshawu, Dipeni, Kanniedood	Mopani, Shingwedzi	69 km ★★★ ★★★★
S51	Sable Dam Road	Letaba	8 km ★★★★
S52	Red Rocks/Tshanga Loop	Shingwedzi, Bateleur	47 km ★★★★

Notes

Road number	Name of road	Closest rest camp	Distance & rating
S53	Nkulumbeni Loop	Shingwedzi	2 km ★★★
S54	Nyawutsi Bird Hide	Crocodile Bridge, Lower Sabie	2 km ★★★
S55	Lamont Loop	Shingwedzi	3 km ★★★
S56	Mphongolo Loop	Shingwedzi, Sirheni	31 km ★★★★★
S57	Link Road–Sirheni	Shingwedzi, Sirheni	5 km ★★★
S58	Loop Road Dzundzwini	Punda Maria	9 km ★★★★
S59	Mandadzidzi Road	Punda Maria	7 km ★★★
S60	Gumbandebvu Road	Punda Maria	16 km ★★★
S61	Klopperfontein Loop	Punda Maria	7 km ★★★★
S62	Engelhard Dam Road	Letaba	15 km ★★★★
S63	Pafuri Crooks' Corner Loop	Punda Maria	23 km ★★★★★
S64	Nyala Loop Road	Punda Maria	7 km ★★★★
S65	Waterhole Road	Skukuza	13 km ★★★★
S68	To Mlondozi Dam	Lower Sabie	18 km ★★★
S69	Nhlanganini Loop Road	Letaba	8 km ★★★
S76	Dirt Loops over H4-1	Skukuza	8 km ★★★★
S79	Low-water Bridge Loop	Lower Sabie, Skukuza	3 km ★★★★
S82	Shortcut to Lower Sabie	Lower Sabie	10 km ★★★

Notes

Road number	Name of road	Closest rest camp	Distance & rating
S83	Marula Loop	Skukuza	7 km ★★★★
S84	Mantimahle	Skukuza	3 km ★★★★
S85	To Olifantsdrinkgat	Skukuza	1 km ★★★★
S86	N'waswitsontso Loop Road	Satara	4 km ★★★★
S89	Link Road to Balule	Balule, Olifants Camp	8 km ★★★
S90	Old Main Road	Satara, Balule	38 km ★★★★
S91	Link Road to S92 Olifants River	Balule, Olifants Camp	5 km ★★★★
S92	River Road–Olifants Camp	Olifants Camp, Balule	7 km ★★★★
S93	Olifants–Letaba Road	Olifants Camp, Letaba	16 km ★★★
S94	Shortcut to Letaba	Letaba	7 km ★
S95	Letaba–River Loop Road	Letaba	7 km ★★★★★
S96	Shilawuri Link Road	Letaba	15 km ★★★
S98	Thulamila Loop	Punda Maria	6 km ★★★
S99	Mahonie Loop	Punda Maria	25 km ★★★★★
S100	N'wanetsi River Road	Satara	19 km ★★★★★
S101	Loop to River Bank	Shingwedzi	3 km ★★★
S102	Mpondo Link Road	Crocodile Bridge, Biyamiti	9 km ★★★
S103	Olifantsbad	Mopani, Shingwedzi	2 km ★★

Notes

Road number	Name of road	Closest rest camp	Distance & rating
S104 (S1)	Albasini Road	Pretoriuskop, Skukuza	4 km ★★★★
S105	Ntandanyathi Bird Hide	Lower Sabie	2 km ★★★★
S106	Rabelais Road	Talamati, Marula, Tamboti, Orpen	14 km ★★★
S107	Nhlanganzwani Road	Crocodile Bridge, Lower Sabie	2 km ★★★★
S108	Link Road	Crocodile Bridge, Biyamiti	2 km ★★★
S110	Berg-en-Dal Loop	Berg-en-Dal	18 km ★★★★
S112	Renosterkoppies Road	Skukuza	6 km ★★★★
S113	Link Road	Skukuza	3 km ★★★
S114	Old Malelane, Skukuza Road	Berg-en-Dal, Biyamiti, Skukuza	52 km ★★★★
S118	Mhlambane Loop	Berg-en-Dal, Biyamiti	8 km ★★★★
S119	Gardenia Hide Road	Berg-en-Dal, Biyamiti	6 km ★★★★
S120	Mountain Road	Berg-en-Dal	8 km ★★
S121	Timfenheni Loop	Berg-en-Dal	6 km ★★★
S122	Muntshe Loop	Lower Sabie	12 km ★★★
S125	N'waswitsontso Road	Satara	20 km ★★★★
S126	Sweni Road	Satara	22 km ★★★★
S127	Link to Timbavati	Satara	9 km ★★★
S128	Old Lower Sabie–Tshokwane	Lower Sabie	32 km ★★★

Notes

Road number	Name of road	Closest rest camp	Distance & rating
S129	Link Road S128 and H10	Lower Sabie	4 km ★★
S130	False-thorn Thicket	Crocodile Bridge, Lower Sabie	13 km ★★★
S131	Phalaborwa–Letaba (Dirt)	Letaba	46 km ★★★
S132	Marhumbini Link Road	Letaba	7 km ★★★
S133	Jumbo Road	Letaba, Mopani, Shimuwini	9 km ★★★
S134	Loop Road around Camp	Shingwedzi	6 km ★★
S135	Low-water Bridge Road	Shingwedzi	4 km ★★★
S137	Duke Link Road	Crocodile Bridge, Lower Sabie	7 km ★★★★
S140	Talamati Road	Talamati, Maroela, Tamboti, Orpen	19 km ★★★★
S142	Shongololo Loop	Mopani	36 km ★★★
S143	Capricorn Road	Mopani	14 km ★★★
S144	Old Road to Shingwedzi	Mopani, Shingwedzi	33 km ★★
S145	Fairfield Road	Talamati	12 km ★★★
S146	Stapelkop Road	Mopani	16 km ★★
S147	Ngotso Road	Balule	7 km ★★★★★

Notes

Additional
Information

PLACE NAMES

Place names in the Kruger National Park reflect the legacy of the diverse ethnic and cultural groups over many centuries that occupied, visited, traded in or crossed the area where the park is today. These groups ranged from Stone Age hunter-gatherers, to tribes such as the Swati, Sotho, Tsonga and Venda, to Arab and Portuguese traders, European traders, explorers of Dutch, Greek, Hungarian, Irish and British origin, hunters (legal and illegal) and Voortrekkers (emigrants who left the British Cape Colony and moved into the interior during the 1830s and 1840s as part of the Great Trek).

The name of the **Balule** Camp was derived from the Tsonga name for the Olifants River, which they called 'Rimbelule'.

Numbi Gate is named after the fruit of the *stamvrug* (stem fruit – *Englerophytum magalismontanum*), which grows in rocky places in its vicinity.

Phabeni Gate was named after the Sotho word for a shelter or a cave and the gate and town called **Phalaborwa** means the place that is better (warmer) than the south, from which the Sotho people originally migrated.

Masorini is the name of a hill near the Phalaborwa Gate and was the name of a Sotho person who once lived where the Archeological Museum is today.

The word **mlondozi** means a strong-flowing stream in Swati. The Mlondozi Dam was built in this stream with the Mlondozi Picnic Site overlooking it. The nearby **Lebombo Mountains** can also be seen from there. The Zulu and Swati call these mountains the *amabombo*, which means the direction one takes when journeying.

The H4-2 runs parallel to the **Vurhami River**; the Tsonga word for 'cold'. The name given to the **Vutomi River** along the S33 means 'healthy and alive'. When the dam was built in the Vurhami Stream, the Swati called this place **Gezantfombi**, which means 'the place where the young maidens bath'.

N'wanetsi is the name given to a seasonal river and also a picnic site after the Tsonga word for 'water that glitters and shines, is clean and clear'. The river called **N'waswitsontso** is so named because of its subterranean nature – it shows itself only here and there. On the other hand, the Swati word for 'good or clean water' is **Mantimahle** and this name is given to a dam, windmill and a seasonal stream.

The name for the **Timbavati River** is derived from the Tsonga term *ku bava*, which means 'bitter or brackish water'. The name given to the **Tsendze River** means 'to wander around like somebody roaming in the bush'.

The **Luvuvhu River** derives its name from *mvuvhu*, the Venda word for the river bushwillow (*Combretum erythrophyllum*). The Tsonga call the thin reed (*Phragmites* sp.) growing in marshy areas *fayi*. Dense stands of this reed are found along the S14 or **Fayi** Loop Road.

Nkaya Pan near Satara is named after the Tsonga name for the knob-thorn tree (*Senegalia nigrescence*), while **Nkuhlu** is the name for the Natal mahogany (*Trichilia emetica*) and **Ntoma** the name of the jackalberry (*Diospyros mespiliformis*). **Ntomeni** means 'the place where this tree grows'.

Sweni means to 'wrap up tightly' in Tsonga, while **talamati** means 'an abundance of water'. The Sweni River, the Sweni Game Viewing Hide and the Sweni Trails Camp are all close to Satara. Talamati Camp is indeed situated in a place where there is an abundance of water.

Distances between camps and gates

	Berg-en-Dal	Crocodile Bridge	Letaba	Lower Sabie	Malelane	Mopani	Numbi Gate
Berg-en-Dal		149	234	113	12	281	97
Crocodile Bridge	149		196	34	141	243	130
Letaba	234	196		162	226	47	216
Lower Sabie	113	34	162		105	209	95
Malelane	12	141	226	105		272	94
Mopani	281	234	47	209	272		263
Numbi Gate	97	130	216	95	94	263	
N'wanetsi	180	142	94	108	170	141	162
Olifants Camp	219	181	32	147	210	86	201
Orpen	213	175	117	141	204	164	195
Pafuri Gate	453	415	218	380	444	172	434
Paul Kruger Gate	83	88	173	53	74	220	65
Phalaborwa Gate	285	246	51	213	277	74	267
Pretoriuskop	92	125	211	90	85	258	9
Punda Maria	415	377	176	342	408	130	396
Satara	165	127	69	93	156	116	147
Shingwedzi	344	306	109	271	333	63	325
Skukuza	72	77	162	43	64	209	54

The table shows distances between Kruger National Park rest camps and gates. If you are planning a self-drive safari to the Kruger National Park, it is important to take note of the gate opening and closing times.

N'wanetsi	Olifants Camp	Orpen	Pafuri Gate	Paul Kruger Gate	Phalaborwa Gate	Pretoriuskop	Punda Maria	Satara	Shingwedzi	Skukuza
180	219	213	453	83	285	92	415	165	344	72
142	181	175	415	88	246	125	377	127	306	77
94	32	117	218	173	51	211	176	69	109	162
108	147	141	380	53	213	90	342	93	271	43
170	210	204	444	74	277	85	408	156	333	64
141	86	164	172	220	74	258	130	116	63	209
162	201	195	434	65	267	9	396	147	325	54
	79	63	312	119	145	156	274	25	203	108
79		102	250	158	83	195	212	54	141	147
63	102		335	152	167	184	297	48	226	137
312	250	335		392	246	438	76	287	109	380
119	158	152	392		224	60	354	104	283	12
145	83	167	246	224		261	201	119	137	213
156	195	184	438	60	261		389	140	318	49
274	212	297	76	354	201	389		245	71	342
25	54	48	287	104	119	140	245		178	93
203	141	226	109	283	137	318	71	178		271
108	147	137	380	12	213	49	342	93	271	

You also need to take into account the distances between camps and gates. This is important as there is a speed limit of 40 km/h on dirt roads and 50 km/h on tar roads within the park.

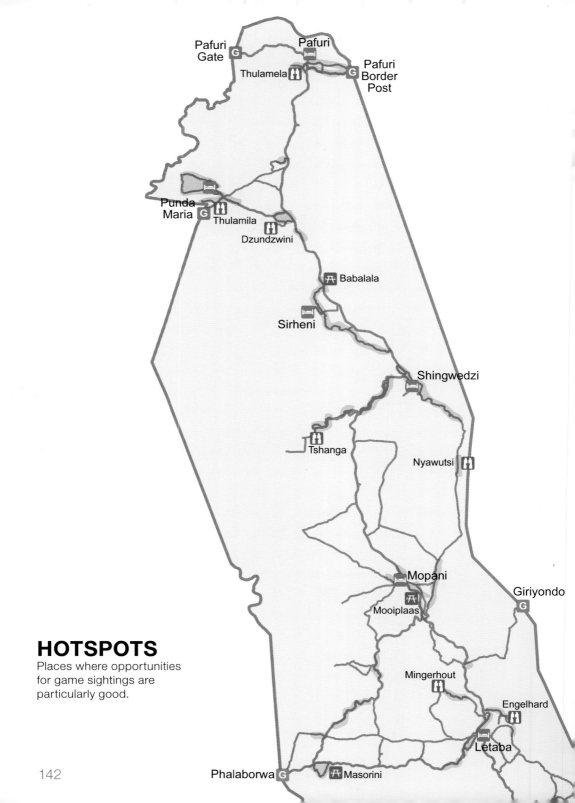

Pafuri
Gate G

Pafuri

Thulamela

Pafuri
Border
Post G

Punda
Maria G
Thulamila

Dzundzwini

Babalala

Sirheni

Shingwedzi

Tshanga

Nyawutsi

Mopani

Giriyondo G

Mooiplaas

HOTSPOTS
Places where opportunities
for game sightings are
particularly good.

Mingerhout

Engelhard

Letaba

Phalaborwa G   Masorini

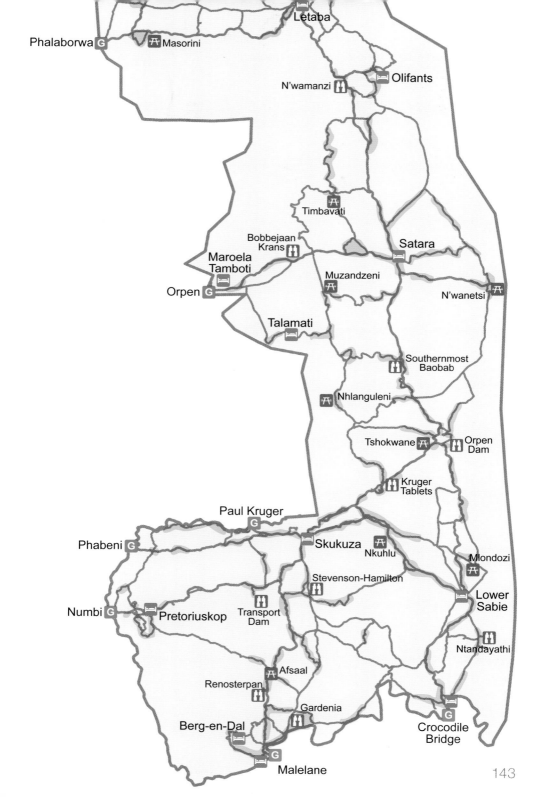

Letaba

Phalaborwa G   🅰 Masorini

N'wamanzi ♟   🛏 Olifants

🅰 Timbavati

Bobbejaan
Krans ♟

Satara 🛏

Maroela
Tamboti 🛏

Orpen G ◻   Muzandzeni 🅰   N'wanetsi 🅰

Talamati 🛏

Southernmost
Baobab ♟

🅰 Nhlanguleni

Tshokwane 🅰   ♟ Orpen
Dam

Kruger
Tablets ♟

Paul Kruger G

Phabeni G   🛏 Skukuza   🅰
Nkuhlu

Mlondozi
🅰

Stevenson-Hamilton

Numbi G 🛏 Pretoriuskop   ♟
Transport
Dam

Lower
Sabie 🛏

Ntandayathi ♟

🅰 Afsaal

Renosterpan ♟

Gardenia ♟

Berg-en-Dal 🛏

Crocodile
Bridge G

Malelane G

143

THE VAN DEN BERGS

The Van den Bergs photograph, write and publish their own books on wildlife and the environment. Their books can be ordered at **www.hphpublishing.co.za**.

Their close association with nature took the Van den Bergs on many journeys of discovery into the remotest parts of southern Africa. Passionate about the environment and wildlife, they spend as much time as possible in wild places, studying the intricate interactions and relationships of plants and animals and keeping a photographic record of their observations. This guidebook is the culmination of practical bush knowledge gained by observation and study over many years.

Copyright © 2021 by **HPH Publishing**
First Edition
ISBN 978-0-6398318-2-4
Text by Ingrid van den Berg
Photography by Philip & Ingrid van den Berg,
Heinrich van den Berg
Publisher: Heinrich van den Berg
Edited by Diane Mullen
Proofread by Margy Beves-Gibson
Design, typesetting and reproduction by
Heinrich van den Berg, **HPH Publishing** and Nicky Wenhold
Maps by Linda McKenzie – Digital Earth, GIS Consulting and Nicky Wenhold
All Geographical Information System (GIS) datasets were obtained from Scientific Services, Kruger National Park, South African National Parks, and have been utilised with permission and according to the requirements of the Data User Agreement.
Printed in China

First edition, first impression 2021

Published by **HPH Publishing**
50A Sixth Street, Linden, Johannesburg, 2195
info@hphpublishing.co.za
www.hphpublishing.co.za